MEDITATIONS
for
MOTHERS
OF TODDLERS
by
Beth Wilson Saavedra

W9-CBE-239

WORKMAN PUBLISHING, NEW YORK

Cover illustration by Lonni Sue Johnson

Library of Congress Cataloging-in-Publication Data

Saavedra, Beth Wilson.
Meditations for mothers of toddlers / by Beth Wilson Saavedra.
p. cm.
Includes bibliographical references and index.
ISBN 1-56305-566-X (pbk.)
1. Mothers—Prayer-books and devotions—English.
2. Devotional literature. I. Title.
BL625.68.S34 1995

306.874'3—dc20   94-21500
                                                    CIP

Workman books are available at special discounts
when purchased in bulk for premiums and sales promotions
as well as for fund-raising or educational use. Special
editions can also be created to specification. For details, contact the Special Sales Director at the address below.

Workman Publishing Company, Inc.
708 Broadway
New York, NY 10003

Manufactured in the United States of America

First printing February 1995

10 9 8 7

To my son, Alexander, who inspires me, sharpens my vision, and strengthens my faith in life. You are truly heaven sent.

To mothers everywhere, value the extent of your contributions and remember the words of Alexis De Veaux: "Motherhood is not simply the organic process of giving birth . . . it is understanding the needs of the world."

Acknowledgments

I am grateful to the following people who have been instrumental in creating this book: Peter Workman, Ruth Sullivan, Robbin Gourley, and Sam McGarrity. Special thanks go to Diane Botnick for her excellent suggestions and inspired prose.

To my father, Paul, who continues to be a steady source of love, laughter, and support, and to my "second mother," Linda, whom I have come to know more deeply: I love you both.

For my love of the written word, I thank my Grandma Mamo and my mother, Anne.

My deepest love and gratitude to my special friends: Jillian Klarl, Linda D'Agrosa, Morgan Soderberg, Nancy Edison, Lee Cook, Todd Nelson, Jessica Donnelly, Ginger Hinchman, Rose Benstock, Betsy Allen, Eric Lieberman *(je t'aime),* Maris Allen, Brad Pearsall, Caroline Douglas, Warren Finch, Marilyn Sierra, Daryn Stier, Nancy Ison, Louie D'Agrosa, Shirley Luna, Pia Hultquist, Liz Lauffer, Linda Urborg, Diana Cope Duffy, Marcie Mitchell, Jeanne Feeney, Elizabeth Hodgins, and Homa Tavana.

Special thanks to the Mountain View Parent Nursery School: Betsy Nikolchev, Claire Koukoutsakis, and Tim Dobbins.

*W*hat a pleasure to be asked to write an introduction for my daughter's new book, *Meditations for Mothers of Toddlers.*

As I write these words, I feel myself standing in the succession of women writers in our family—women who wrote and were also mothers. There was my great-grandmother, Mary Elizabeth, a pioneer woman who probably never even had the chance to consider herself a writer, and yet she wrote beautiful letters. I especially remember one I saw that she had written to her only daughter, Maudie, who at eighteen was many miles away and about to give birth to her first child. My great-grandmother was sleeping in a barn as she and her husband were traveling across the West in a wagon. My grandmother, Maudie, never received that letter as she died in childbirth.

My mother, Manilla, was mothered by her grandmother and grew up to be a writer. As a young girl, she was busily producing short stories and poetry and had been given a scholarship for college when the Depression hit. She made the decision to give up her writing in order to support her grandmother throughout the Thirties. Like so many women, writing then became something she did on the side and juggled with being granddaughter, then wife and mother. She became a published poet before she died.

I came kicking and screaming into writing. I had never conceived of myself as a writer—I was a talker. But writing *Meditations for Women Who Do Too Much* was like giving birth to a bright, energetic child who took off on its own and continued to spawn spin-offs.

My daughter, Beth, followed the tradition, combining the two professions of motherhood and writing. We all know how the tension between motherhood and finding time for work and art can result in our feeling like a high-tension wire at times, which Beth deals with in this book. When our life demands that we spend so much time caring for others, it's difficult to see sometimes that our needs, as mothers, as people, fall through the cracks.

They say that prostitution is the oldest profession. I doubt it. I think that mothering is, and it is truly the most important profession a culture can have. All of us have been mothered (probably not the way we *thought* it should have been done), and mothering is key in everyone's life, whether it be mothering or the lack of it. In our lineage of mother-writers, we have all done both as best we could.

There is no one right way to mother. Each mother has her own personality and every child has a particular personality also. Often the best things we do are also the worst things we do and vice versa. Ultimately, the most important gift we can give our children is the gift of ourselves and being present to them.

Yet, mothering can be a lonely time, a lonely place. So often we are "on our own" with it. We are no longer surrounded by the tribe or extended family, and often the only company we have are other mothers who are struggling too. It helps to share our struggle, and it helps to have a little companion such as *Meditations for Mothers of Toddlers* to carry with us.

Meditations for Mothers of Toddlers follows the usual form we have come to expect from meditation books: Each entry begins with a quotation by a wise person—some are famous, some are not. This quotation is followed by some words of reflection on the quote. These reflections can challenge, inspire, comfort, or tickle. Then comes a summary, a jumping-off statement, which we can take with us as a companion through the day or the next five minutes. The meditations are brief, as they should be when geared toward women with little time.

These meditations do not deign to tell mothers

what to do—mothers get enough advice as it is. What with parents, grandparents, other mothers and society-at-large all knowing what mothers should be like, if there's one thing mothers don't need, it is another advice-giver. These meditations are intended to participate with you. They will make you laugh, or cry. They will stir up feelings, comfort and challenge. They may change your perceptions or relieve your anxieties. They may feel like open arms or a tumble in the surf. Hopefully, they will be just what you need when you need it.

I am grateful to be a part of this mother-writer lineage and privileged to write this introduction to my daughter's new book. Indeed, mothering comes in many forms.

Anne Wilson Schaef, Ph.D.

Soothing Rhythms

Every single human being was drummed into this world by a woman, having listened to nine months of heart rhythms of their mother.

CONNIE SAUER

Rhythm is essential to all life. After our baby is born, he rests peacefully on our chest, breathing along with the steady beat of our heart. Growing older, he begins creating rhythms of his own: stomping feet, pounding drums, or clanging spoons together.

Although our young child ventures out into the world by day, he still seeks the comfort of our lap at night. He enjoys leaning against our warm body and being lulled by the pulsing music of our heart. We hold him while rocking in a chair or swinging in a hammock and feel ourselves return to our own rhythm.

Through my body I give my child life, and through my body I give him the love of rhythm that is the pulse of life.

*In an age when we are told that good mothering is
just a matter of finding the right sitter and learning
how to arrange "quality time," most of us could
never have envisioned how completely we would be
taken by these delicious miniature people.*

LINDA BURTON

any of us planned our lives well in ad-
vance. Whether we embarked on successful careers or followed our creative urges, we
certainly didn't expect a little thing like having a
child would so alter our lives. Then we discovered
how wrong we were. How could we have known
that we would become so attached to "these delicious miniature people"?

While some of us took leave of our jobs, others
opted to cut down on hours spent away from home
or to convert a garage into a home-office. Why did
we make such sweeping life changes? Because we
discovered that we had needs *as mothers*.

**Now that I know how much being a mother
means to me, I will gladly arrange the rest of my
life around it.**

The human animal needs a privacy seldom mentioned, freedom from intrusion. He needs a little privacy as much as he wants understanding or vitamins or exercise or praise.

       PHYLLIS McGINLEY

*E*very one of us desires privacy. It doesn't matter whether it's an office away from home or a room of one's own, as long as it has a door to close. Here we can allow our minds to wander and our bodies to relax and know our solitude will not be interrupted. As my good friend Shirley once commented, "Just once I'd like to go to the bathroom without someone disturbing me. No, better yet, I'd like to go to the bathroom without having to announce it."

While it doesn't matter where we take our privacy, it does matter that we take it.

Would I deprive myself of food? No. Then why deprive myself of privacy?

There are only two lasting bequests we can hope to give our children. One of these is roots; the other, wings.

🏵 HODDING CARTER

*B*eing a mother means we must build a solid foundation for our child and help him develop the tools to be independent. It's a delicate balancing act: knowing when to help and when to allow him to help himself. Often a push-pull ensues. Our child insists he can do something himself, pushing us away one minute and the next whining, "Mommy, help me," as if we've thoughtlessly abandoned him. Our child's confidence shifts like sand in the desert—and we shift with it.

It is important to remember that this dance in which we engage with our child has a purpose. Each step, forward or backward, is a move toward sprouting the wings he will someday need to take off on his own.

The love and security I give to my child will enable him first to take root and then to take wing and soar.

It is dangerous to confuse your children with angels.

🍦 DAVID FYFE

When we first contemplated motherhood we may have pictured smiling angelic faces adorning spacious homes, but it didn't take long to be disabused of that fairy tale. Our living quarters are most likely still cramped. Our children are angelic only when sleeping, and they can get pretty devilish during the day.

But imagine our toddler never having a bad moment. What if she always smiled and ate all her dinner and spoke only when spoken to and left no ring in the bathtub? What would be left for us to do?

Angels make boring children and demand perfect moms, too. I will gladly tackle the challenge of my little human.

To keep a lamp burning we have to keep putting oil in it.

          🚲 MOTHER TERESA

While it is not impossible to love our children twenty-four hours a day, it *is* impossible to extend our love twenty-four hours a day. Many of us try, but we give out too much for too long, and the result is burnout. Then, we have *nothing* to give. With our resources so depleted, we can't generate the energy it takes to express our love, and everyone loses. We feel bad about having so little to give, and our child feels bad because there is so little to receive.

I am a loving mother. But if I hope to be a constant source of love and affection, I must spend some part of each day giving to myself.

You may have a wonderful child. Then, when he's thirteen, gremlins carry him away and leave in his place a stranger who gives you not a moment's peace.

JILL EIKENBERRY

e know these gremlins start paying us visits much earlier. Usually at age two our child experiences his first dramatic change in personality. He is moody and willful and often unleashes full-blown temper tantrums. The tantrums subside as his emotional development starts lining up with his verbal acuity, and it's as if our child is returned to us.

But we mustn't get too comfortable. Around age three, the gremlins return. Once more, we are faced with "a stranger who gives us not a moment's peace." He is demanding and not easily placated.

After a cycle or two, we catch on. It's assuring to know that our child's psychic structure is torn down and replaced about every six months. Doubly assuring to remember that he is secure enough in our love to express his most confused and vulnerable self.

Being a mother means that I receive the best my child can give and, sometimes, the worst.

Regression

Seeing you sleeping peacefully on your back among your stuffed ducks, bears and basset hounds would remind me that no matter how good the next day might be, certain moments were gone forever.

🍦 JOAN BAEZ

Children aren't the only ones who regress. We mothers go through periods of longing for the baby vanishing right before our eyes. We want to keep on using his last baby word and feel almost betrayed when he suddenly learns the right pronunciation. We celebrate his independence, yet feel rejected when we find we can no longer kiss him in front of his friends.

Like a flash of lightning penetrating our psyche, we realize that certain moments are gone forever. We find ourselves asking, "Am I ready for this?" Yet all the while we know that our child's developmental victories are upon us, ready or not.

Certain moments are gone, but I will treasure them forever.

Life shrinks or expands in proportion to one's courage.

&ช ANAIS NIN

*T*hose of us who have several children probably found that we needed to put ourselves temporarily on a shelf. Many of our personal plans have had to come second or third for quite awhile now. But, for whatever reason—sending our youngest off to school, hiring outside help, our husband taking on more—we are beginning to know that it's time to step down off that shelf. Sometimes, this is a frightening prospect.

We must first reacquaint ourselves with the person we used to be, and then consider how much we've changed. When we see how much more we are now, we will know we are ready to take on the world.

Life doesn't happen on a shelf. I will find the courage to step down and dig in.

A friend is a gift you give yourself.

☙ ROBERT LOUIS STEVENSON

So many different kinds of friends grace our lives. There are the ones we've known since childhood who probably still envision us with missing front teeth and pigtails. There are the ones we met in college with whom we traded clothes and boyfriends and intimate late-night confessions. There are those we met at work who know our professional selves and who've added an extra dimension to "talking shop." And there are the ones we've met as moms. They love our children, we love theirs, and we spend so much time together that it becomes difficult to tell where one family begins and the other ends.

No matter how long we've been together, whether we speak once a year or every day, each of our close friends has a special way of knowing us. And through them we see different aspects of ourselves.

My closest friends are gems. I am richer for having them be a part of my life.

Ritual is the original womb of art; its waters continue to nourish creativity.

MARIAM SIMOS

Isn't it sad when a personal ritual—one that's taken years to perfect—becomes just another item on our long list of things to do. It's then that we begin to discount them, telling ourselves that they can wait, letting more pressing matters come first. Yet we'd never expect our children to do without their bedtime stories, their tickle time, or their afternoon "talk" with their bear.

Our rituals provide an anchor to our days. For some of us that means rising before the kids to read the newspaper and sip our coffee. For others, it's a hot, scented bath after the kids have gone to bed, or a monthly night out with the girls. And when we think we're too tired, maybe we'll just settle into the couch for a dose of T.V. Instead, we must remind ourselves how cheated we'd feel. The fact is, rituals give more than they take.

My daily rituals must not be hurried or skipped. I must instead depend on them to renew me.

Different Rules

Some social niceties bite the dust when you're a 90's working mom.

⏋ ANN BANKS

*P*otluck dinner! We eagerly accept, but with some trepidation. First, our plans for an early exit from the office are thwarted. Then when we get home, everything that can go wrong does. We shake our heads in despair. Other people work, we know. Our friends who are single or mothers of grown children will manage to arrive beautifully dressed and carrying elegant dishes. We long to make similarly impressive entrances.

But those of us with young children know that when it comes to social graces, we operate under different rules. We're allowed to bring paper plates and napkins instead of food. We don't have to have neatly wrapped packages, and we know that the party will continue even though we're a little late. Eventually, if we ease up on our unrealistic standards and contribute what we can, an evening with friends will be more entertaining than trying.

My friends understand how stretched I am for time and energy, and so must I.

Our culture . . . seems to have forgotten the importance of fathering and to have divorced manhood from fatherhood.

🐾 RICHARD LOUV

Some of us have husbands who want to participate more fully in child rearing. However, many of them haven't a clue about how or where to start. And we're part of the problem.

Our husband may be reluctant to assert himself knowing he'll be held accountable if the Dad-size portion of dessert he served leads to sugar-madness, or if a bout of roughhousing leads to bumps and bruises and cries for Mom.

It is essential that we mothers learn to step out of the way. We must allow our partner to fumble through the good *and* the bad on his own. Sharing our experiences can help, but when he is free to test his own routines and establish his own rapport, a father learns, a child learns, and so do we.

My toddler's needs can be as easily satisfied by Daddy as by Mommy. I need to step back and give my spouse a chance.

Stages

When you are dealing with a child keep all your wits about you, and sit on the floor.

🍦 AUSTIN O'MALLEY

A two-year-old insists: "It's mine! It's mine!"

A two-and-a-half-year-old cries: "No!"

A three-year-old moans: "Moooooooom, I can do it."

A three-and-a-half-year-old bellows: "I want everyone to do what I say."

A four-year-old puffs out his chest and exclaims: "I'm the strongest. I'm the fastest. I'm the smartest."

A four-and-a-half-year-old yells: "I'm Master of the Universe!"

And we mother them all!

Sometimes I feel as if my child is fast-forwarding his way through life. I can't slow him down; all I can do is enjoy the show.

Sharing

There are two things a child will share willingly—communicable diseases and his mother's age.

        ℆ BENJAMIN SPOCK

When our child is a baby everything is his, including Mommy. "Mine, mine, mine" rings in our ears as we coax him to let a friend touch his truck or share a moment of our attention. One day, though, we notice that the struggle takes on a new dimension. He doesn't really *want* to give up his truck, but he understands that it's more fun to share toys with his friends than to play alone. We've witnessed one of those great leaps. Now he wants to show off his new skill offering us everything from dripping ice-cream cones to antiquities he's dug up from between the couch cushions.

Teaching our child to share is a long process, and the rewards are sometimes more than we anticipated.

Cooperation

The essence of pleasure is spontaneity.

☙ GERMAINE GREER

There are times when we throw our cares to the wind and let our child take the lead. We let her choose the games and the food and the activities. We accept any part she assigns, and not only do we play our character's role to the hilt, but we let the game go on and on until it finds its own end. What a surprise to suddenly look at the clock and discover it's time for bed; what a delight not to have to face bedtime battles and to look forward to the next day together.

When I cooperate with my child, it allows her to see that doing what someone else says isn't always a win/lose situation. Sometimes it's fun!

Learn to say "No"; it will be more use to you than to be able to read Latin.

🖉 CHARLES HADDON SPURGEON

No! A staple in any home with toddlers. She will test our "No" at every turn. But we know its value. When her safety is on the line, it's easy to hold firm. However, many situations arise that are less clear-cut yet demand an on-the-spot response. Sometimes after we've said "No," we may rethink our decision. Perhaps we've been too impulsive or arbitrary and the next time, we determine that our response will be different. Then our child grows and her new capabilities change the entire scenario so that today's "No" becomes tomorrow's "by all means."

"No" is a very important word. I will use it with confidence. I will use it sparingly.

Even the most courageous warriors need to remember this simple wisdom: there is a time to take on the world and a time to rest, replenish and reflect.

JILLIAN KLARL

We don't tend to think of ourselves as warriors. Warriors take on the world; we rarely go beyond the confines of our neighborhood. Warriors have titles; we are merely Mom. And warriors are the stars of the nightly news, while we conduct life in relative obscurity.

Yet what if the cameras were turned on us? They'd reveal the peace talks we conducted throughout the day; the children we counseled; the surgery performed on a broken toy; and the protection and encouragement we've provided to our troops.

Even the President escapes to Camp David now and then, and we, too, need R & R. As all good warriors know, balance is essential to being effective in the world—wherever we choose to serve.

I don't expect medals for my years of duty, but I do deserve rest and time for reflection.

Shared laughter is erotic too.

🌾 MARGE PIERCY

*R*emember how, back in high school, your body used to thrill with excitement whenever someone you *really liked* made you laugh? The laughter itself seemed to cut through all the tension and awkwardness, and your body tingled with the possibility of passion.

As adults, we tend to forget the pleasurable eroticism of laughter, the kind of uncensored, spontaneous laughter that suspends drudgery and tension. Perhaps we need to take time to feel the release of real, heartfelt laughter—even in front of the kids!

Laughter is another way of coming together for mutual pleasure.

Compassion

Compassion for myself is the most powerful healer of them all.

🍦 THEODORE ISAAC RUBIN

As mothers, we're quick to lavish others with compassion but rarely remember to save any for ourselves. When our child spills a drink on the carpet, one look at the panic in his eyes and our irritation dissolves. We assure him that it's okay and show him how to hold on to his cup. When he falls and scrapes himself, we acknowledge his hurt and offer Band-Aids and comfort. When he moves into a new situation, we don't push him. We stand by him, waiting for the cues that he needs our help, and then step in.

Why can't we do the same for ourselves? Because we're adults? Where is it written that adults must be all-knowing, immune to hurt, and infallible? Not in this book!

If I allow my innate compassion to extend to myself, I will be more forgiving of my mistakes.

Suffer not to teach the child, for knowledge acquired under compulsion has no hold on the mind. Rather, find the natural bent that the child may learn.

                            PLATO

Children are naturally curious. Their minds delight in everyday wonders as they piece together the puzzle of their world. They touch a butterfly's wing and want to know why dust comes off on their hands. They see the sky illuminated and are challenged by the concept of electricity. They catch a bug in a jar and, with the intensity of a biologist, observe its behavior. To keep this sense of wonder alive, they need to be able to share their observations with an adult.

We feel fortunate to be that adult. It's a relief to know that we don't have to force our own information on our children but can urge and encourage them to uncover their own.

Learning is a joyful process. I will follow where my child's curiosity leads.

. . . Remember that your authority is not based on being right. It is based on who you are . . . You are the one in charge. That's the way it's supposed to be.

🌹 PEGGY O'MARA

We like to think that if only we take the time to explain ourselves properly reason will prevail with our youngster. But for every reason we come up with for doing something—and he will make us go through them all—our four-year-old devises startlingly articulate counter-reasons. Wracking our brain to remember some persuasive tactics we learned in our child development course, we call up the words our instructor guaranteed would work. She stumps us again—as if she's in law school, not preschool. No longer concerned about being right or even understood, we resort to the tried-and-true, "Because Mommy said so." Let her find a comeback to that!

It's my child's job to question my authority; it's my job to maintain it.

Choosing Battles

Now who is to decide between "Let it be" and "Force it"?

🍦 KATHERINE MANSFIELD

*L*eaving the house in the morning puts us all to the test. We race against the clock, our child defies it. We put out his bowl of cereal and cut up the fruit just the way he likes it, and he decides it's a pancake kind of day. We could argue, but in the interest of time, we grit our teeth and stir the batter. Then he insists on wearing his Ninja Turtle swimming trunks to preschool even though it's snowing. And if we have the presence of mind to suggest that he wear the trunks *over* his sweatpants —a strategem that finally gets us out the door and into the car—he decides to boycott seat belts. At this point it's our call: will a little more tactical maneuvering save the day or merely delay an inevitable confrontation?

We learn to sense when skillful diplomacy will smooth the way and when the battles must be fought.

Mom, I have to say shut up. It's in my nature.
          ALEXANDER SAAVEDRA

*O*ur child comes up with all kinds of ways to bend the rules. His first attempts may be clumsy and obvious, but over time he becomes surprisingly adept. His vocabulary grows along with his sense of power and daring. If he doesn't like our ruling on a request, he'll seek a second opinion—or even a third—and then so confidently quote his higher authority that we're almost tempted to reconsider. As a friend once said of her three-year-old, "It's difficult to tell which one of us is smarter!"

Anyone who gets a good chuckle out of us certainly deserves a break; congratulating his ingenuity may be wiser than giving in, however.

I will set boundaries and my child will constantly test the limits of these boundaries. Together, we will shape a family policy.

Sleeping Alone

Just like my two-year-old, I wanted to shout, "It's mine! It's mine!" every time the kids demanded to sleep in my bed.

🦌 SHIRLEY LUNA

We try everything in the book to get our baby to sleep in her own bed. Finally, we enjoy a few peaceful, uninterrupted nights alone with our husband. Soon we begin to count on sleeping through till morning. Then nightmares and monsters rear their ugly heads and our child is back. Only now, she takes up much more room, she kicks harder, she steals all the covers, and, adding insult to injury, she snores!

For the first night or two my husband and I may laugh about our predicament. But after a few nights out on the couch, nothing seems funny. It's hard to know when the terrors have subsided and habit has set in. But we know that to get our nights back, we must act fast.

Once our bed is returned to its rightful place of privacy and intimacy, my husband and I will do whatever we can to keep it that way.

There cannot be a crisis next week. My schedule is already full.

HENRY KISSINGER

Our schedules have never been more jam-packed. A son needs valentines for his class party; a daughter needs to be carpooled to her swimming lesson; a baby needs to go to the doctor; a friend needs help planning a surprise party; a project is due at work, and everyone needs new shoes. We do our best to prioritize, but it seems as if everything must come first. There are weeks, even months, when we simply cannot fit one more thing into our schedule—not even a crisis!

To simplify my schedule, I must be willing to say yes to what is truly important and no to everything else.

Why does everyone lose it when I have a "bad day"?

🚲 SHIRLEY LUNA

O ur families depend on us in ways that they (and sometimes we) rarely realize. They draw energy from us—a kind of invisible force that, in many ways, centers them and keeps them buoyant. On days when we are unable to give out this seemingly constant flow of energy, however, they think we're withdrawing from them.

We may be accused of "being in a bad mood" simply because we aren't supplying the juice for their batteries. And frequently even we label these as "bad days," when what we are really doing is reserving energy for ourselves. There's a difference between withdrawal and inner recharging, and we and our family need to recognize this difference.

I will teach my husband and child that when I go into myself I am not going away from them.

I don't know everything. I just do everything.

🦋 TONI MORRISON

*O*ur middle name is "Efficiency." Our incredible knack for organizing extends far and wide. We become so skilled at "keeping it all together" that we end up doing the majority of the work simply because we don't give anyone else the chance to do their share.

While efficiency is an admirable trait, it can take its toll on everyone. We might try loosening up and letting a few things slide. We may be surprised that the world doesn't stop when the kitchen sink fills with dishes. An even greater surprise may be that another set of helping hands can do the job just fine!

There is such a thing as too much efficiency.

Sex is hardly ever just about sex.

🍦 SHIRLEY MACLAINE

S ex is often not about sex. Sometimes it can be used to express anger. At its worst, it can become a tool of power and control. However, at its best, sex is mutually healing and exciting. It connects us to ourselves while it connects us to another.

Yet, how often do we take time to reflect on our own sexual needs and desires? How often do we ask for the touch we want? Maybe it's time to decide what we want from sex and ask for it.

Sexuality is central to my life. For my well-being, it's important to make wise choices about its use.

Part of my plan has been to pleasantly remind adults of what they were themselves, and how they felt and thought and talked, and what queer enterprises they sometimes engaged in.

🚲 MARK TWAIN

*T*he magic of childhood can slip away from us adults. When our child turns over the furniture to create a castle, we may not see the castle for the chairs. Sometimes, we must suspend practical considerations for the sake of experimentation—those enchanting, clever, childhood enterprises. After all, our child is creating a world—his own. And if we're lucky, we just might get invited in.

When my world becomes too "real," my child's ingenuity will bring back the magic.

*You can remember the second and third and the
fourth time, but there's no time like the first. It's
always there.*

🦋 SHELAGH DELANEY

*A*s a friend once reminisced: "To have a first
child again . . . " She was thinking back to
the time when her daughter was her only focus—
before the two boys came along. She didn't have to
respond to multiple demands from other children.
Instead, she basked in the simple motherly pleasures of breastfeeding, napping together in the middle of the day, taking quiet strolls through the park.
She cherishes those enchanted interludes with her
baby and regrets the fact that she can't give such
undivided attention to her younger children.

Like her, we all worry that our youngest will get
the short end of the stick or our firstborn will feel
left out. It may be impossible to meet everyone's
needs, but an occasional date alone with each child
can work wonders.

**I will enjoy my children to the fullest even
though I can't lavish the same undivided
attention on each of them.**

────── *Perspective* ──────

Parenthood is a kind of death . . . We're afraid of the death of our individuality, when it is really our selfishness that dies . . . We're afraid of the death of our childlikeness, when it's really our childishness that dies . . . A major initiation of parenthood is this letting go of our false self so that our real self can shine forth.

🍦 JOYCE AND BARRY VISSELL

*E*very time we encounter new mothers, we remember: how we never took our eyes off our infant, how we were always touching her, always second-guessing her needs. We would forget to comb our hair or eat. Our entire focus was on our baby.

And our toddler is even more involving. Now we must monitor the worlds through which she moves, the information she processes, the friends she makes. Yet paradoxically, it is this intense focus on another that forces us to strip away the superfluous and hone in on what really matters. All our choices and decisions—no matter whom they concern— bring us closer to our authentic self.

Sometimes, when I move the farthest away from myself, I get the clearest perspective of my life.

We are each other's reference points at our turning points.

&ailable; ELIZABETH FISHEL

No matter what it was like growing up, an entirely new relationship begins once sisters have children. No more the big sister or the "baby," we're both experts now. We go to each other for guidance and advice. We look to each other for encouragement. As we raise families of our own, we welcome the opportunity to reflect on our own childhood with someone who shared it. If there was no bond then, there is now. And, if we were already close, we become closer. Thanks to our children, we have the opportunity to reestablish old ties, only this time as adults, as mothers, and as friends.

In motherhood, my sisters and I share a common thread—a thread that draws us together and transcends our differences.

In literature as in love we are astounded by what is chosen by others.

🐌 ANDRE MAUROIS

We make choices that baffle our friends. Our friends' choices, in turn, baffle us. "How could she have married that man?" we think. "Why doesn't she hire a nanny to help with her twins?" we wonder. "How could she have quit law school when she was first in her class?" we ask ourselves.

The fact is, our lives look and feel totally different from the inside. A choice that seems impulsive to someone else may in fact be the result of years of contemplation. A friend's partner may lack social skills, but in the privacy of their home may provide her with the kind of unquestioning support she needs. Being human, we're bound to have opinions about others' lives. If we want to remain friends, we must leave judgment to a higher authority.

I don't have to understand my friends' choices; but being a friend means I accept them.

Apples and Oranges

Recently my fingers have developed a prejudice against comparatives. They all follow this pattern: A squirrel is smaller than a tree; a bird is more musical than a tree. Each of us is the strongest one in his own skin.

BERTOLT BRECHT

For some of us, our first child was a breeze. He ate and slept according to schedule, smiled at every given chance, and we congratulated ourselves for being such good mothers. Then, along came our second—a child so different in temperament, so full of testing that our mothering skills seemed rendered useless.

For some of us, it was the other way around. Our first cried incessantly no matter what we did, and we began to think that we'd never get relief. We forged ahead, and to our amazement our second child turned out to be a gift who made us understand why women keep having babies.

Our children will continue to weave in and out of phases, and we will be constantly surprised by their differences. Of course, we will compare them. But more, we will celebrate the uniqueness of each.

I will trust in my own abilities as I mother two very different individuals.

Mom, you're a robot.

🚲 ALEXANDER SAAVEDRA

*H*aving a perceptive child means not being able to get away with anything. He knows when we're present, just as he knows when we flip on the automatic pilot and turn into Robot Mom.

Whenever we let our checklists take over, our child goes on the alert. For him deadline is just a word. Schedules are mere guidelines—rough ones, at that. Rushing is a concept foreign to his very being.

All of us have external demands that put pressure on us, and we need to remember that a hectic lifestyle not only takes us away from ourselves but makes us less available to our child. He needs what robots can't give: love and attention.

It is important for me to feel a sense of accomplishment and equally important for me to remain emotionally available.

*Jarrell was not so much a father . . . as an affection-
ate encyclopedia.*

🏺 MARY JARRELL

*A*s mothers, we offer what only a mother can
give. By the same token, what fathers offer
is also unique. Not only do our children receive the
composite of our family traits—our love of poetry,
sports, walks in the rain—they also benefit from
our individual strengths. For instance, one parent
may not be particularly helpful when it comes to
comforting tears, yet when it comes to teaching
children how to work crossword puzzles, she's the
best. One parent may not always know the football
scores, but when it comes to naming flowers, he
can't be beat.

**I will celebrate the unique contributions both my
husband and I make to our children's growth.**

They lie on their noses at first in what appears to be a drunken slumber, then flat on their backs kicking and screaming, demanding impossibilities in a foreign language. They are human in nature in essence, without conscience, without pity, without love, without consideration for others—just one seething caldron of primitive appetites.

🍦 KATHERINE ANNE PORTER

Children are "out there." They make few attempts to conceal their true feelings, whether they're enraptured or enraged. Social graces and other people's sense of propriety mean little to them. They are passionate in their desires and passionate in their fury. Their words and reactions are honest, immediate, and deeply felt. They do not yet know the yoke of restraint, and they bubble away like a "caldron of primitive appetites." If we do not keep too tight a rein, we can help our runaway colts harness their energies without discouraging their enthusiastic pursuit of life.

My child exhibits the raw emotions of being alive. My job is to help her find the most creative avenue for her energies.

It's clear that most American children suffer too much mother and too little father.

🚲 GLORIA STEINEM

*E*ven those of us with husbands who share in the duties of household and child rearing find ourselves on our own when it comes to the emotional issues: Is my son ready for preschool? Why does my daughter seem so sad these days? Is my son more aggressive lately because of T.V., or is there something else going on? We tend to keep these worries to ourselves. Maybe we fear that our husband won't feel our concern. Maybe he'll say we're overreacting, or worse, make a quick judgment without weighing all the facts.

On the other hand, if we try not to second-guess him, we just may discover a partner to worry along with. When we give him something real to sink his teeth into, emotional housekeeping can be a shared activity.

If I don't spare my husband the emotional trials of raising our child, he will be there to help sort out more than the laundry.

*Every person needs recognition. It is expressed
cogently by the child who says, "Mother, let's play
darts. I'll throw the darts and you say 'wonderful.'"*
                                🎀 M. DALE BAUGHAM

hildren not only need our attention, they
demand it. "Mommy, watch . . . Look at me,"
they practically scream in our faces. And if we think
we're too busy to respond, we'd better think again.
Our loving attention is most desirable, but in a
pinch negative attention will do. Attention is attention.

We know, for ourselves, how vital it is to receive
praise. It is as necessary as sunshine, rest, and good
food. It is heart-and-soul sustenance, and without it,
our spirit withers. But we also know the importance
of small gestures. Our husband gives us a spontaneous hug, our boss suggests we take the afternoon
off, a friend listens to our stories. We feel rewarded.
And when we recognize our child in small, loving
ways, he'll feel rewarded, too.

**The attention I give my child need not always be
elaborate, but it must be constant.**

Children aren't happy with nothing to ignore. And that's what parents were created for.

🍦 OGDEN NASH

e've all been warned, but it's still a shock when our child first realizes that he can avoid doing our bidding simply by ignoring us. "Honey, please put on your shirt so we won't be late." No response, not even a flicker. We try again, "I really need you to put your shirt on, now." Is it his ears? We try again, raising our voice. "If you can't do it yourself, I can help." Still no response, and worse, he shuffles off just out of reach.

Do we try a hearing test—asking if he'd like a cookie, perhaps? Or do we get down to his level, look him right in the eyes, lock him between our knees, and pull on the shirt ourselves?

No one likes to be ignored. I will find more creative ways to get around my child's passive resistance.

Tensions grew at home and my work suffered as I committed to tighter and tighter deadlines.

ELLEN SUE STERN

*D*eadlines at work crash in on us. We are recruited for another school project, unanticipated crises come up and only we can handle them. The load of responsibilities is too great for any one individual to finesse, yet we wonder why we can't take everything in stride. Sometimes we make mistakes; other times, we fail to follow through. It's terrible to feel that we've let our family down, especially since all we've been trying to do is make their lives better.

When we find ourselves in these situations, it is time to zero in on what we can do. We learn to say, "I can't decorate the entire classroom for the visit with Santa, but I can buy ornaments for others to hang up," and we all benefit.

When I complete a manageable task, I feel a lot more rewarded than when I leave more ambitious tasks undone.

The Doldrums

We are making hay when we should be making whoopee, we are raising tomatoes when we should be raising Cain, or Lazarus . . . Spend the afternoon. You can't take it with you.

🐾 ANNIE DILLARD

We all fall into ruts. Our schedules fill up and we have little room for flexibility, much less spontaneity. We long for change, but the mere thought of it exhausts us. There are so many people to consider now. We feel bound to weigh everyone's happiness and often end up pleasing no one.

But, what if we tried changing only our own lives, even though they are inextricably bound with our family? What if we pursued something just for ourselves? What would happen? Perhaps we would discover that our family would come to appreciate the infusion of new ideas and new energy. Perhaps we would discover that they, too, have tired of the doldrums and want change.

When one person in a family changes, it gives the others a chance to change, too.

Housework can kill you, so why take a chance?

PHYLLIS DILLER

We hate those times when the level of our housekeeping begins to mirror our life: Nothing ever stays put. Sometimes we manage to close our eyes to it, but when we find ourselves looking for the same thing for the third time in a day, it's hard to keep one's cool.

Wouldn't it be nice to be able to step over toys on our way out the door without giving them another thought, or to feel comfortable walking the grocery aisles in our best clothes because we haven't had time to do the laundry, or not mind that our child has decided to try out her new markers on that important document? Not in this lifetime.

I like a clean house and I value my sanity. Maybe I could settle for a little bit of each.

Men have been trained in the importance of single-mindedness. Women, on the whole, have not had the privilege of single-mindedness. Instead, women have had to learn to be attentive to multiple demands; to think about more than one thing at a time. This skill is absolutely essential in the modern world.

🚲 MARY CATHERINE BATESON

*O*ur baby cries to be fed. Our oldest wants help with her homework. The "middle child" can't find his favorite program on television. In unison we hear, "Mom!" But we can't possibly be in three places at once.

One by one, we tackle the issues that arise, constantly prioritizing and juggling each child's needs until everyone is tended to. And, when appropriate, we provide guideposts that will help our older ones meet their own needs without our assistance.

If God was a woman, She would have given mothers eight hands.

Whether you're a woman or a man, when you're out there fighting the world, you want to come home and find peace.

🎗 JOHN H. CLARKE

*P*eace in a houseful of young children is hard-won. Children always seem to be in motion. Their mouths are as active as their bodies. When we return home from work, longing for a little peace and quiet, we are besieged by bouncing children, eager to share stories and laughter. They need our laps and our loving attention.

Hopefully, we can nab a few moments, after our children have gone to bed, to bask in the stillness of the house before we, too, drift off to sleep.

Part of being a parent is learning how to find moments of peace and accepting that these moments may not always be available.

The cure for anything is salt water—sweat, tears or the sea.

ISAK DINESEN

ealing comes in many forms. When stress has invaded our bodies and we are restless, even in our sleep, we usually need to sweat. Running, swimming, climbing, any exercise that energizes our bodies will do. When we are feeling disconnected from ourselves and the natural rhythms of life, we need to go to the healing waters of the ocean and allow ourselves to be lulled by her endless ebb and flow. And when we are feeling sad, we need to cry, copious, saltwater tears.

Water can be my source of healing and strength.

A Child's Dignity

Feel the dignity of a child. Do not feel superior to him for you are not.

🚲 ROBERT HENRI

No one likes to be looked down upon. No one likes to be spoken to as if he's inferior. Yet we are occasionally guilty of treating our children without the respect they deserve. Perhaps we're in a rush and we order our children into the car. When we tell them to "buckle up," our youngest begins to cry. His tears merely irritate us further. "What is wrong?" we snap at him, only to discover that he can't yet manage the seat belts in our new car. He feels hurt and we feel intense remorse. Luckily, we can still apologize, gathering together our own dignity and giving our child a chance to regain his.

To treat my child with dignity, I must keep my own intact.

I didn't want to be rich. I just wanted enough to get the couch reupholstered.

KATE MOSTEL

For mothers, success can be a double-edged sword. While it is satisfying to sell our works of art, run our own business, or make senior partner, greater success brings greater demands.

Shifting our preoccupation away from our child is bound to be confusing for both of us. She may feel the need to compete for our attention, while we need our downtime more than ever.

Rather than resenting "Mom's work," our child can learn to take inspiration from it. New schedules for us mean new schedules for her, and the diversity can be exciting. And when we bring home evidence of our day's work, she learns to share the pride we take in our accomplishments. As one child proudly announced, showing off a picture he was painting, "Look Mom, I'm doing my work, too!"

All aspects of my work reflect who I am.

I am open to receive with every breath I breathe.

MSIA SONG

s mothers, we are so accustomed to giving that we often forget how to receive. Our preschooler brings home an art project that she made for us, and we congratulate her on her accomplishment rather than thank her for her gift. Our partner presents us with an armful of roses for no particular reason, and we find ourselves trying to pinpoint what we did to earn them.

Whenever we catch ourselves feeling uncomfortable on the receiving end of life, we're probably feeling unloved, unworthy, and undeserving. We need to remember that the members of our family love us for who we are, not simply for what we do. And they enjoy expressing their feelings and their gratitude.

When I am open to receiving, I am open to love.

But to look back all the time is boring. Excitement lies in tomorrow.

🚲 NATALIA MAKAROVA

*O*utings with young children can be fraught with anticipation. When we go to great lengths to plan a trip to the museum, we may expect too much of our child. Instead of being excited by all the new sights, he ends up bored and unenthusiastic. We return home wondering, "Was it worth the effort?" Then, a few months later, we return to the same museum, only this time, inexplicably, everyone has a grand time. We are pleased yet puzzled. When we replay the event in our mind, we can't figure out why this trip was a success and the previous one a disaster. Perhaps lowering our expectations is the key.

Though I know it's a gamble, I will keep venturing forth because, when we have a good time, we *really* have a good time.

I stay in marvelous shape. I worry it off.

🖎 NANCY REAGAN

*A*s mothers, we spend a great deal of time redirecting our child's focus. Instead of simply saying "No," we are skillful in shifting our child's behavior from negative to positive. For example, when our child is bouncing on the couch or frantically running around the house, we visit the park, where she can work off some of that excess energy. If she is tired and restless, we introduce play-doh or water games, or read a soothing story.

But when we're at wits end, do we think about using these same techniques on ourselves? Maybe the next time we find ourselves worrying we can ask our child if we might borrow some of her play-doh to knead. It may take a few minutes, but eventually, if we focus on our hands instead of our mind, we, too, will lose ourselves in the activity.

Worrying throws me off-center. I need to restore my calm through simple activities.

So why can't I
Do like papa do,
Like papa do,
Like papa do now.

🍦 JOE TEX

emember admiring someone so much you wanted to dress and talk and walk just like her? Our children are no different. To them, we adults are fascinating and glamorous, and they will go to great lengths to be just like us. They see Daddy wearing cowboy boots and want to stomp around in their very own pair. They insist on accompanying us to the hairdresser and taking their turn under the dryers. They come to our office, swivel around in our chair, and "work" at our computer. If imitation really is the sincerest form of flattery, then flatter away, we say.

I hope my children will always find me worthy of imitation.

When is a toddler no longer a toddler? When a confusing, unpredictable and balky person-in-the-making becomes a comparatively cooperative and recognizable human being who is both eager and easy to please—at least 50 percent of the time.

                                          PENELOPE LEACH

s Penelope Leach can attest, the quantum leap in a child's development takes place somewhere around the age of three. And most often the changes catch us quite unprepared.

For instance, when our child was little, everyone could roam the house naked. Now we find he is paying more attention to our bodies, making observations as well as comparisons to his own. We may feel embarrassed but also reluctant to abruptly "cover up." How do we convey a sense of appropriateness without imparting the wrong message about the human body? One way to do that is to avoid focusing on nudity when the real issue is privacy. That's something he can respect *and* understand.

Doing what comes naturally in my home will have to change and evolve along with my child. I will watch for the signals.

If at first you succeed—try to hide your astonishment.
🌿 LOS ANGELES TIMES SYNDICATE

*M*any of us have whole libraries of books on parenting, yet we've remained skeptical of their contents. Isn't it amazing when a situation seems to cry out for one of those pearls of wisdom; we try it and it actually works the first time! For example, we've done everything we can think of to make our child stop at street corners. We've warned him about the dangers; we've insisted on holding his hand; we've even yelled at him in public. Then, we decide to follow the instructions in one of our books: "Make it fun," it says. "Walk briskly up to the street corner and jump in the air while saying 'stop!'" The next thing we know, our child has become an expert at crossing the street, and at every opportunity he reminds *us* to watch out for cars!

I'll do my best not to look too astonished if I succeed on the first try. There's a lot to be said for garnering and testing those pearls of wisdom.

The scientific theory I like the best is that the rings of Saturn are composed entirely of lost airline luggage.

👂 MARK RUSSELL

*Y*oung children ask a lot of questions, probing questions. And their earnestness calls for thoughtful, accurate answers. Yet, on occasion, we just don't have the answer. We don't even have enough information to fudge it. It's during these moments that the poet in us takes flight. Before we know it, we are spinning out fanciful answers that have more truth than fact. We are delighted. Our child is skeptical. "That's not the right answer," she charges. "You made that up."

Then remembering our instructions about telling the truth, she hits us with a real showstopper: "If you make up a story, are you lying?" We weren't prepared this morning to engage in a philosophical discussion about fiction and truth. Where's that poet when we really need her?

To answer my child's questions I must rely on knowledge, imagination, and, most of all, a sense of humor.

When I first became a mother I made the mistake of assuming that to follow my own heart's desire was in direct competition with being a good mother. I'm glad to say I was wrong. Dead wrong.

🚲 LISA RIDDLE

"The only way to be a good mother is to sacrifice," we may start out thinking. However, it doesn't take long before we discover that being a mother and "following our heart" need not be mutually exclusive pursuits. Indeed, they may actually complement each other—making us better mothers than we would have been had we abandoned those things we love.

I will trust that I can bring *all* of who I am to my mothering experience.

Sometimes a cigar is just a cigar.

🐾 SIGMUND FREUD

*A*nalyzing our child is a necessary part of learning who she is and how she responds to the world. When we know what's behind troubling behavior, it is easier to change it. So it's natural to look for the causes of tantrums and moodiness.

But when we feel insecure about our mothering, we begin to question everything, blowing things completely out of proportion. "Could she be crying because I left her with my mother all day yesterday?" we ask ourselves. "Is she basically an unhappy child?" we worry.

When I find myself overanalyzing issues of minimal importance, it's helpful to remember that, sometimes, "a cigar is just a cigar."

Body Image

I haven't got the figure for jeans.

🍦 MARGARET THATCHER

*I*sn't it amazing how much our bodies change with time? With every birth of a child, our bodies take on a new shape; a fuller, more womanly figure. Our hips round, our breasts expand then shrink. Our tummies develop a soft crescent as lovely as the sliver of a new moon. Our arms and legs are firmer and stronger from all the lifting and carrying. This maturing into motherhood fits us just fine—whether we fit into jeans or not.

My body is a testament to motherhood. I will relax into its new fit.

Every child is an artist. The problem is how to remain an artist once he grows up.

🚲 PABLO PICASSO

C hildren are naturally creative. Their drawings spring from the same seemingly endless font of originality as their thoughts. They weave together perceptions of the world in ways that defy logic and rationality. To them, all is real. By the age of four they begin to sense that there are boundaries to their physical reality. "Is that really real?" we may hear them ask, yet they seem still to understand that "real" is a relative term. Unless they are taught to limit their inner vision— which has happened to most of us—they remain in touch with the expansive creative force as a fact of everyday life.

Irrepressible and unsocialized, my child reminds me how I feel when I am most alive.

The ache for home lives in all of us, the safe place where we can go as we are and not be questioned.

🌺 MAYA ANGELOU

*E*very one of us needs a home, a safe place where we can be at ease, a safe place where we feel accepted for who we are. Some of us came from homes that felt loving and comfortable. While others came from homes where we had to protect ourselves and hide our deeper inner stirrings.

As mothers, we have a second opportunity to create a true home, not only for our children, but for ourselves as well. Although our actual living quarters may not always meet our ideals, it's important to remember that home is where we feel loved and respected. Home is where we are gathered up into the circle of people who enrich our lives.

Home is more than a physical structure. It is the essence of love in which I encircle my family.

I wonder if anyone else has an ear so tuned and sharpened as I have, to detect the music, not of the spheres, but of earth, subtleties of major and minor chord that the wind strikes upon the tree branches. Have you ever heard the earth breathe?

🍦 KATE CHOPIN

ike dolphins, children have a heightened sensitivity to the world around them. They detect the music in nature and dance to its symphonies. They take on others' moods. Criticism feels as sharp as the prick of a needle. The scent of flowers is inhaled through their every pore. They "hear the earth breathe." And for them the world is a wondrous place.

As mothers, we have the opportunity to nurture this sensitivity. And, instead of encouraging our children to toughen up or deny what they feel, we can help them find constructive ways to express their sensitivity.

My child senses more in one week than some people do in a lifetime. Let me share in his gift.

I always wanted to be somebody, but I should have been more specific.

          LILY TOMLIN

We always knew we wanted to be somebody, and we may have been quite specific, but the birth of our child changed everything. We thought we'd be satisfied with a maternity leave, but now we want to quit our job. Motherhood once seemed an incidental part of life, but no longer. Everything must be reconsidered. And after a few years at home with our child, questions like, "Who do I want to be?" are soon replaced by "Who am I?" How do we lead a life that takes both our aspirations and our need to be with our children into account?

Life is like a road trip. It's good to start out with an itinerary, but it's the detours that get really interesting.

. . . the creative woman seeks an equal partner, a companion, a soul mate, someone who shares her values, interests, and particularly an understanding of the meaning of her work.

🌸 CLAUDIA BEPKO AND JO-ANN KRESTAN

*M*arriage can be a supportive partnership based on cooperation and self-expression. When we're both feeling comfortable as a team and secure in our own identities, an easy give-and-take spirit infuses our home. We cook dinner and our partner automatically cleans up. We go to pick out our child's pajamas and return to find her intently listening to the bedtime story being read by her father. When neither of us has to say, "It's your turn, I've done it three nights in a row," new avenues of communication open up. We stop blaming our partner for our discontent; he stops blaming us for his. Instead, we strive to accommodate each other's needs and feelings. Respect that starts in the home follows us wherever we go.

Respect is basic to every true partnership. I'm fortunate to have such a fulfilled relationship.

I'm suggesting we call sex something else, and it should include everything from kissing to sitting close together.

🍦 SHERE HITE

e live in a culture that so narrowly defines sex it leaves out everything but intercourse. And as most women know, intercourse is only one part of lovemaking. There are times when the intimacies of hand-holding, hair-stroking, and caressing words can be gratifying in themselves. When we broaden our definition of sex to include the joy of sensual communication, we discover how often we *are* loving with our husband. We stop worrying about the frequency of intercourse and realize, instead, that we're making love—whether it's with our hands or words or eyes—all the time.

If I define sex in a limited way, I limit the pleasure available to me in every touch.

I was born modest, not all over, but in spots.

&⅋ MARK TWAIN

oung children can change so suddenly. As toddlers, they freely run around the house blissfully naked. Even outside, we're likely to catch them stripping off their clothes before we can cross the yard to stop them. Then, one day, it happens: They ask for their own changing room at the clothing store (calling us in to button them up). They demand privacy when using the bathroom (calling us in to wipe their bottom). In short, they become modest—sometimes all over, sometimes in spots.

My child will go through stages of modesty. I will try to keep up and respect his growing need for privacy.

*Parenthood remains the greatest single preserve of
the amateur.*

ALVIN TOFFLER

In her writings, Lynn Andrews describes two
types of mothers: Earth Mothers and Rainbow
Mothers. Earth Mothers are usually close to home.
They have meals prepared on time. They handle
the needs of their children throughout the day in an
orderly fashion. While not rigid, they allow for few
surprises. On the other hand, Rainbow Mothers
rank solitude and their own pursuits up there with
caring for their children. Their daily schedules are
flexible, and meals may be eaten in the car if it buys
a little more time at the fair.

We shouldn't waste a lot of time trying to determine which we are. Most of us are a combination
and go through cycles of being one or the other.
And even if we are primarily an Earth Mother or a
Rainbow Mother, one thing is certain. We're living
proof that children flourish within a variety of styles.

**Whether I'm a Rainbow Mother or Earth Mother,
my child will benefit from my personal style.**

To mention a loved object, a person, or a place to someone is to invest that object with reality.

ANNE MORROW LINDBERGH

College, career moves, and marriage have taken many of us far from our original homes. For a time, being on our own is liberating. But once we have children, we realize the importance of family. We want our child to know who we are and where we came from, to have a sense of history and heritage, to have roots.

Though annual visits "home" may not be enough to make this connection, our family can be a strong presence in our child's heart and mind. When we talk about the aroma of Grandpa's pipe, our child can smell it. Adventures with our beloved dog, the winter light that streamed through our bedroom windows, the music of Great-grandma's old country stories all are made palpable. And when we make them real for our child, we are reminded of how important they are to us.

Talking about the people and places I love is the best way of keeping them present in my heart.

Differences

All children smile in the same language.

🚲 BUMPER STICKER

O ur child notices everything—especially differences. "Why does that girl have red hair?" she wants to know. "Why does that man have a gold tooth?" "Why does Grandma have wrinkles all over her face?" She wants to understand why everyone is not just like her. She is intrigued by the variation in individuals that we either take for granted or learn to avoid. Rarely does she attach judgment to these differences. When people smile at her, she smiles back. Then her curiosity takes over. She stares or asks questions and we find ourselves apologizing for her. We may have to endure the embarrassment, however, because without these awkward explorations she will never come to understand and celebrate the amazing differences that make up her world.

My child is curious about the diversity among people. My answers to her questions will help her to shape ideas about what she observes.

Good Days, Bad Days

I'm a wonderful person; I never said I was easy to live with.

ANONYMOUS MOTHER

*L*iving together as a family means we get to experience the full range of each other's moods. Some days, we awake cheerful and energetic and our most loving, tolerant side shines forth all day. Other mornings, we can tell, on getting out of bed, that we'd better put up the "beware" sign. Our crabbiness only increases with each rough patch. The only consolation is knowing that just because we have "bad days" doesn't mean they eclipse the wonderful person we are.

No one is easy to live with all the time. Not even me.

When you and Dad argue, I feel mean inside. I feel like I want to hurt somebody.

☞ ALEXANDER SAAVEDRA

*R*emember how it felt? We'd be tucked away in bed, the house would get quiet, and then the arguing would start. Whether the problem was serious or not, our parents' fights would sound frightening and leave us lying awake dreading the inevitable: divorce. As grown-ups, we know that every fight doesn't lead to separation and that every family does quarrel. And airing our disagreements can provide a normal and healthy release.

But unless we want our child lying awake at night, afraid and uncertain, we must heed the frequency and intensity of our arguments. Words leave lasting impressions, especially with a child. Of course, it's best to talk out problems before tempers flair. But when that's not possible, we must teach our children that sometimes it's okay to disagree, settle our conflicts, and move on.

When I express my anger in less hurtful ways, my child learns that healthy argument is a part of life and not something to be feared.

I love it—I love it, and who shall dare
To chide me for loving that old arm-chair?

🚲 ELIZA COOK

*O*ur lives can get us chugging along like machines, and most of us assume we can go on running forever. But machines break down, and so do we, without care and maintenance.

When we forget what proper care and maintenance means, we can look to our child. We know his needs better than our own. We know he needs comfort, for instance, and so do we. And like him, we need the touch of other human beings. We need the warmth that radiates from others' hearts. We also have needs of our own, like the soothing sound of water, sun on our face, breeze ruffling our hair. And when our bones are weary, we need to collapse into the comfort of our "old arm-chair."

I will take refuge in the arms of my love, the arms of my friends, and the arms of my chair.

His voice was as intimate as the rustle of sheets.

🐸 DOROTHY PARKER

Having a child can temporarily put sex on the back burner. While we may think wistfully about the intimacy and lovemaking we used to share, we realize we cannot "produce it at will." Rather, we must respect its flow in the larger scheme of our lives. As one mother put it, "This sexless period is just a phase. If I'm not too impatient with the future and can accept that I am temporarily 'treading water,' it won't be too bad."

For couples with children, sex is a little like getting on the proverbial bicycle. A turn or two around the block will bring it all back.

In America sex is an obsession. In the rest of the world sex is a fact of life.

MARLENE DIETRICH

*I*t is easy to become obsessed with sex when you don't have much. Raising children often takes so much time that we rarely have the chance, though often the desire, to be passionate. We envision erotic interludes that, like romantic movies, skip all the bothersome details like finding a babysitter and buying the birth control.

Next time we fantasize about hot, rollicking sex, we should grab the moment—whether it's a morning shower à deux or a drop-in "lunch" at our husband's office.

Just because I can't always be spontaneous about sex, doesn't mean I can't, on occasion, be as wild as I used to be.

If a child lives with approval, he learns to live with himself.

🚲 DOROTHY LAW NOLTE

Some of us worry that our child seems always to hold back. She is timid and reluctant to try new things. Sometimes, because she is not the squeaky wheel, we fear her needs will be overlooked. We see her classmates jumping out of their seats to respond to the teacher, and we wish our child were less passive.

Though a certain amount of reticence is age-appropriate and no cause for worry, our shy child will need our help as she makes the transition from home to the outside world. Listening to her reactions and encouraging her to talk about her feelings will help her grow more confident. After all, "if Mom thinks what I have to say is important, maybe other people will, too."

My child may not be ready to express herself in front of strangers, but I can help by letting her know that what she has to say is of value.

*Our daydreams—and our nighttime dreams as
well—can allow impossible wishes to come true. And
they can, in fact, make a difference in how we feel.*

JUDITH VIORST

No one can do everything, and after we
have a child, it seems as if we can do very
little. For many of us, having to put our dreams on
hold is a much greater sacrifice than all the caretaking, sleepless nights, and loss of autonomy. We wait
and wait for the opportunity to return to our dreams
when we could be focusing on ways to realize
them, bit by bit.

We may not be an award-winning painter overnight, but we can turn a room into a studio and
lock the door for a couple of hours on weekends.
We may not be able to return to college full-time,
but one course a semester can eventually lead to a
degree. Coming to terms with the fact that we can't
do everything doesn't mean giving up our dreams
entirely.

**If I allow my dreams a chance to guide my days, I
can make them real.**

Lovers don't finally meet somewhere. They're in each other all along.

🍦 RUMI

*L*ittle did we know what would await us that moment our child was conceived. But once this little stranger came into our lives, it was as if we were looking at a face we had known forever. This love is a miracle, at once simple and complex, demanding and gratifying, frightening and awesome. As each year passes, our child's personality becomes more defined and we are struck by the unique individual we see emerging. The more we get to know him, the more we seem to love him.

It is difficult to imagine life before my child. I have always been his and will always be his.

No one can sufficiently capture in words the euphoria, the gratitude, and the total delight which can follow a natural birth. The "high" of these moments is spiritual to the utmost, while remaining utterly physical.

🚲 QAHIRA QALBI

Some of us had a difficult or disappointing first birth. Perhaps an emergency C-section was performed, and we felt we lost the chance to bring our baby into the world naturally. Or, maybe we allowed physicians and nurses "to run the show" and, when it was all over, we felt like it was "their delivery," not ours. Our second time around, we want to make sure we are in charge. Our partner attends birthing classes with us. And we practice coaching and breathing, and try to prepare for every eventuality. We feel calm, clearheaded, and we make sure that even if a C-section becomes necessary the decision, ultimately, will be ours. It will be our own participation in creation.

This time around, my husband and I will experience every aspect of birth.

Toddlers are more likely to eat healthy food if they find it on the floor.

🎀 JAN BLAUSTONE

Some of us may have been proud of our gourmet babies (the ones who'd eat anything from chicken livers to avocado). But now that we have toddlers, we're boasting of only one thing— the most finicky eater. Tales of food fiascoes take over every conversation. There's the one about the mother who'd hide vegetables in the mashed potatoes, and by the time her child had finished picking out every tiny pea, the potatoes were unappetizingly cold. There's the mother who painstakingly sculpted a Mickey Mouse face out of fruit only to hear her son cry plaintively, "But Mommy, I can't eat Mickey!" And there's the couple who finally decided that a balanced meal had been achieved when one of their kids ate a handful of broccoli stems and the other a plate of buttered noodles. Maybe if we set their plates on the floor . . .

I cannot force my child to eat wholesome food. But if I make it available, all will balance out in the end.

Making Friends

One of the quickest ways to meet new people is to pick up the wrong ball on a golf course.

BITS & PIECES

laygrounds are a lot like golf courses. If our child picks up something that doesn't belong to him, he's sure to make a new acquaintance. "That's my truck!" we hear, as the owner comes running. "Can I play with it?" our child asks. "No," the owner replies, at which point our child, holding on for dear life, looks to us for help. We try our best to smooth things over, reminding him about "special toys" and how hard it is to share them; and the owner's mother joins in, coaxing her son to give ours a turn. But, even before we can finish, the kids run off together, new friends, headed for adventure.

I meet people under most unusual circumstances. And so will my child.

If you are in the water with a dangerous shark, swim normally, not excitedly, and try not to bleed.

🚲 SIGN AT THE SAN FRANCISCO AQUARIUM

others are notorious for stating the obvious. "Be careful on that slide. It's a long way down." . . . "Hold my hand, this is a busy street." . . . "Don't touch the stove, it's hot."

In order to keep our child safe from harm, we must repeat the warnings over and over. Our young one grows weary of our constant reminders (almost as weary as we), yet it takes a long time before the information sinks in. Milk still spills, and so does our child. That is why we're always nearby, helping her along until she becomes steadier on her feet. But it never really stops. Long after playground rules have become second nature, we'll be shouting down the road, "Drive carefully!"

My child does not yet grasp the concept of danger. It is up to me to teach her how to protect herself, even when she thinks I'm being overcautious.

Have some sympathy . . . put me down easy . . . I'm a cracked plate.

🦋 ZORA NEALE HURSTON

*I*t is common for women to feel more sensitive at some times than at others (men also have emotional cycles, though they're not as easily charted). We may find ourselves crying over the "reach out and touch someone" commercial or taking the most minor criticisms to heart. Life seems so overwhelming that we wish for a shoulder to cry on—someone who'll listen to our woes without telling us how to solve them. We need to be cuddled and caressed. We need to be loved.

It's okay to feel fragile. And if I let myself ask for it, I may even get the loving attention I need.

We were such a good
And loving invention.
An aeroplane made from man and wife.
Wings and everything.
We hovered a little above the earth.
We even flew a little.

YEHUDA AMICHAI

Although our toddler has begun to make fewer physical demands, he seems to need more and more of our time and emotional energy. The puzzles are trickier, the art projects messier, and every activity requires detailed explanations.

Fortunately, our partner is there to step in. We watch him welcome the conversations we've been side-stepping and we smile. They set off together on a weekend of errands and we feel the relief. Our partnership gives us a needed break. It also gives us one of our more lasting images, the two people we love most sharing the simple pleasures of a day.

When I trust the partnership my spouse and I have invented, our love is multiplied.

*The entry of a child into any situation changes the
whole situation.*

🚲 IRIS MURDOCH

*I*sn't it amazing how we used to embark on an
adventure at a moment's notice? Being prepared meant having a tent and a thick paperback
novel. Now it means children's Tylenol, bug spray,
teddy, a month's supply of disposable diapers and
lots of snacks—and a call ahead for the names of
local pediatricians doesn't hurt.

We're sure we've thought of everything, but then
our toddler pees in his sleeping bag and spends
the rest of the weekend in ours. Rain ruins the
firewood, so we resort to lighting the old propane
stove, which nearly explodes, singeing our hair
and charbroiling the marshmallows. Are we having
fun yet?

**I need to ask myself one question before
camping with my kids: Can I keep my sense
of humor beyond the first day?**

The relation between man and nature is like that between the embryo and its placenta. The placenta nourishes, supports and sustains the developing embryo. It would be quite bizarre if the embryo were to seek to destroy this protector organism.

Michio Kushi

Young children have a natural affinity with nature. They enjoy dabbling in streams and lying in the grass. They climb trees and rush at the ocean's waves, roaring in response to a kind of primordial urge. It is up to us to strengthen our children's bond with the earth, to teach respect and love for the planet that supports life, including their own.

Fortunately, we live in a time when conservation, recycling, and ecology are in vogue. It is now considered "cool" to be concerned with the earth's limited resources. However, if we are to instill in our children a deep sense of responsibility for the earth's care, we must show them that our commitment is long-term and not just a passing fancy.

It is not enough to talk about my values. I must live them.

A mother is not a person to lean on but a person to make leaning unnecessary.

DOROTHY CANFIELD FISHER

*P*raise is as necessary to a child as water to a plant. We want our child to know how proud we are of her and her accomplishments. But some of us don't know when to stop. We frame every drawing. We quote every observation. Our intentions may be good, yet the result is often not what we intended. Instead of encouraging our child, our words invade her activity. Instead of contributing to her work, we interrupt the spontaneity of her creativity.

When we insist that she share all her play and learning with us, it is no longer hers and she will grow to depend upon our approval to validate everything she does. That leaves our child with two options: pleasing us or rejecting us. Either way, we both lose.

I will learn ways of supporting my child's projects that don't take away from her own pleasure in them.

True conversation is an interpenetration of worlds, a genuine intercourse of souls . . .

        THOMAS MOORE

Remember the days when our child was too young for anything but the simplest conversation? How we longed for adult repartee. Now that he has moved into a new level of verbal mastery, we find ourselves having a real conversation for the first time. What our child has to say actually engages us, and we listen and respond in a totally new way. How thrilling, this meeting of minds and the "interpenetration of worlds."

To join together in conversation with my young child is to experience the gift of intimacy.

What do we live for, if it is not to make life less difficult for each other?

🌸 GEORGE ELIOT

hen we add a new member to our family, it's important to find ways to help our older children to feel included in caring for the baby. Asking them to pick out an outfit or a pair of booties for the baby or encouraging them to make funny faces to entertain our little one makes them feel proud to be a "big brother" or a "big sister." Congratulating them for brushing their teeth without help or putting away a game unprompted tells them that we love them and appreciate them for being capable and responsive young people. And if they know they can have our lap all to themselves after baby's bedtime, the wait becomes a little easier.

If I include my child by making him an active part of my new baby's life, he'll feel more comfortable in his role within the family.

Treat people as if they were what they should be, and you help them become what they are capable of becoming.

🍦JOHANN WOLFGANG VON GOETHE

I remember reading an excerpt from my son's preschool handbook reminding parents that one of the more significant functions of attending school in the early years is "to assist children in developing good social skills." And, as we all know, that means so much more than simply getting along with other kids. In a class with others his age, our child has the opportunity to experience respect, brotherhood, and a sense of community. (The ABC's are a bonus.) He discovers responsibilities and tasks that fill his day with purpose. And, hopefully, he will carry a spirit of dignity as he grows and ventures out into the world.

Once my child gets his first taste of being treated like a person, not my baby, he will be more likely to pass along that sense of respect to others.

We told our kids that Toys "R" Us was a museum and we could only look, we couldn't leave with anything.

       🚲 MARCIE MITCHELL

inancial pressures often compel us to devise ingenious strategies for *not* spending money. We pass an ice-cream shop and instead of giving the last of our cash to the man behind the register, we appease our children with a stick of sugarless gum while mumbling something about "doctor's orders." We take our kids to Toys "R" Us and let them examine every toy on display, assuring them that "museums" are just for browsing. Or we might establish a price limit before entering the store, allowing each child to buy whatever he can find that falls within his budget!

I will make shopping a game by finding ways to let my child make decisions within set limits.

Worry

*With any child . . . one hunts for signs of health, is
desperate for the smallest indication that the child's
problems will never be important enough for a
television movie.*

🌺 DELIA EPHRON

*D*uring the toddler years, our child's strengths
become more apparent. And so do her
weaknesses.

Perhaps she has difficulty with her speech or
expresses her anger too freely. We worry that her
social skills are awkward and she needs help
approaching other children her own age. Whatever
issue our child faces, we face with her.

Small problems, we suspect, will become big
problems without our guidance. But we worry
about how to provide that guidance. Do we step in
to assist and risk drawing attention to her shortcomings, or do we wait on the sidelines, hoping she'll
outgrow them? People tell us to stop worrying,
which is a little like telling a bird to stop flying.

**If I trust my instincts and gather the necessary
information, I can be assured that my "worry"
will be productive.**

*The walks and talks we have with our two-year-olds
in red boots have a great deal to do with the values
they will cherish as adults.*

🍦 EDITH F. HUNTER

J remember when I was fourteen, standing in
the kitchen washing dishes with my step-
mother, Linda. She was drying. Soon, the comforting routine and the sound of clinking glasses led
her to talk about similar times she had spent with
her mother. "We'd have the best talks while we
were doing simple things. Somehow, we felt comfortable discussing things that, at other times, felt
too uncomfortable."

I knew exactly what she meant. Sometimes the
very ordinariness of an activity with our child allows
the two of us to open up to new possibilities. During these times, in the enchanted moment, the difficult things, the important things are expressed
without reservation.

**I can turn boring routines into cherished
moments by seeing them as times to exchange
feelings and mind-stretching ideas with my child.**

Our baby-sitter arrives, and they head off to the park. Casey carries a wineskin of water in case he gets thirsty. "So long, Shish Kebab," he says as he leaves. For some reason he is calling me Shish Kebab this week. Last week, it was "Killer Squid." I go upstairs to mull this over.

🚲 MARNI JACKSON

Young children come up with the strangest and most imaginative nicknames. One week our three-year-old addresses us with a bow, calling us "Mommy-san." The next week he refers to us as "Watermelon Towel." And the week after, it's something even more farfetched.

At first we may be perplexed. Then, bemused. It's evident that our child is simply trying out his burgeoning vocabulary, stringing words together that have pleasure or meaning for him. Maybe, we'll be able to decipher their meaning, or maybe we'll find that their only meaning is in the moment.

I will take my child's many names for me as terms of endearment.

Do you love me because I'm beautiful, or am I beautiful because you love me?

🏵 OSCAR HAMMERSTEIN II

No one takes more delight in our children than we do, with the possible exception of their grandparents. There are times when they are so adorable we can hardly contain ourselves. They dig into our makeup and apply our green shadow under their eyes, our reddest lipstick across their cheeks, and eyebrow pencil everywhere. To us they're Birds of Paradise; to others they look more like battered children. They perform our favorite Beatles' songs, knowing every word but struggling to hit those high notes. We're thinking *Wunderkind*, our friends are thinking "tone deaf."

If we noticed the discrepancies we might care, but in our case, ignorance truly is bliss.

My children are beautiful in their own right. The eyes of a loving mother make them even more beautiful.

*. . . a child should not be denied a balloon because
an adult knows that sooner or later it will burst.*

🖋 MARCELENE COX

*W*e all experience times when we're out of
sync with our child. He's riding high, and
we let the air out of his tires. Maybe we're too intent
on completing our daily list of things to do. "Mom,
look at my magic wands," our child says. "Put my
pens back where they belong," we reply. "Can I
wear my special super-hero gloves to the park?" he
asks. "You'll ruin my oven mitts," we insist. Disen-
chantment is written all over his face, and we feel
like The Wicked Witch of the West.

Fortunately, the most amazing thing about children is their resilience. A smile brings us another
chance. We hand our child the balloon he wants,
just because he wants it. Who knows? Maybe this
time it won't burst.

**When pragmatics threaten to take over my day,
it's time to lighten up.**

*Let us accept truth, even when it surprises us and
alters our view.*

🚲 GEORGE SAND

*I*nsight can come at the most unexpected
times. When we try to have a conversation
with a friend, for instance, and our child interrupts
us, we feel quite justified in soundly reprimanding
her. Mommy needs her time, after all. However,
watching our husband scold our child for the same
thing gives us pause to consider. We know how she
has looked forward to having her father come
home from work. We know how unfair it is for him
to expect her to wait for the attention she needs.
Have we been unfair, too?

**Watching others respond to my child allows me
to be more objective about my own interaction
with her.**

*There was only one terrible night when Casey lost his
personality. It was the only time I have seen him
overtaken, unable to muster his usual humor. He
was so exhausted that whenever he was awakened
by the cough, he would glower at me or mutely kick
me in the leg.*

MARNI JACKSON

We've all gone through it. A childhood illness that consumes our lives. Whether
it's whooping cough or an ear infection, our child
becomes our entire focus. Our husband, our other
children, and even work take a back seat. Not only
must we monitor our young one's progress, but we
must also endure the cries in the night, the temper
tantrums over "yucky" medicines, the fits of boredom. And we must be ready with cold compresses,
story books, and love. Then, as suddenly as it
began, the illness subsides and our child is ready for
us to change from nurse back to playmate. It
shouldn't come as a surprise that our child bounces
back to normal more quickly than we do.

**Tending my sick child can be an intense
experience. I, too, will need time for recovery.**

I always felt that the great high privilege, relief and comfort of friendship was that one had to explain nothing.

KATHERINE MANSFIELD

A friend who knows what we need without having to ask is like no other. Our lives are so intertwined that we sense each other's needs and respond accordingly. She knows when to take our children off our hands, and we know when she needs a bouquet of flowers or a home-cooked meal. We share books and secrets. And when our lives take us in different directions so that we fall out of touch for a time, no one's feelings are hurt. Nothing has to be explained. We know we will always pick up where we left off. What a privilege it is to know and be known by someone in this way.

The ease I feel with my closest friend is like no other. With her, I am comfortable being myself.

A good marriage is one which allows for change and growth in the individuals and in the way they express their love.

🚲 PEARL S. BUCK

*A*ny marriage must keep pace with the changes that occur in the two partners involved. But once a child is introduced, the course of change is amazingly unpredictable. Our schedules change, our aspirations change, and how we express our love changes, as well.

Before, a morning kiss could lead to spontaneous, sunlit lovemaking. Now, it's often our child's kiss that starts our day. Our love is often directed to our young child, and by the end of a day our reserves of affection run low. For a time, we seem to need only companionship and friendship. But instead of always looking outside of the home, we might try looking to the friend we have in our spouse. That way we stay close. And when our child is older and we have more time, those concupiscent stirrings that initially brought us together will get their chance to stir again.

I will remember that my husband and I are lovers, partners, *and* friends.

*God is really another artist. He invented the giraffe,
the elephant and the cat. He has no real style. He just
goes on trying other things.*

🐾 PABLO PICASSO

Trying to explain God to our young child is
like trying to explain earthly politics to a
Martian. Whatever we say provokes another, more
challenging question. And no wonder. We, too,
have questions about the mystery of God that *we*
can't answer. Whether we have been struck with
awe at the beauty of God's creation or have felt the
presence of God in our heart, we may find it difficult to convey in words what God means, despite
our desire to pass on a spiritual legacy to our child.

We might try to start small—sharing observations,
pointing out the wonder of God's majesty through
art and animals and music and nature. In these
ways our child may feel the presence of God in her
and around her.

**There are many ways to God. By sharing my
beliefs I will help my child find her own way.**

Acceptance is not approval, consent, permission, authorization, sanction, concurrence, agreement, compliance, sympathy, endorsement, confirmation, support, ratification, assistance, advocating, backing, maintaining, authenticating, reinforcing, cultivating, encouraging, furthering, promoting, aiding, abetting or even liking what is . . . Acceptance is saying, "It is what it is, and what is is what is."

🍦 PORTABLE LIFE 101

*A*ccepting certain life phases can be difficult. We have days or even weeks when we wish circumstances were different. Feeling unable to change things, we dream of great escapes: a trek to Tibet, a singing debut.

Granted, we don't have to like what is. But, if we don't accept what is, we will lose valuable time waiting for magical transformations and remain mired in our reality.

Until I accept what is, I can't begin to change it.

I will praise thee: for I am fearfully and wonderfully made . . .

🚴 PSALM 139:14

*I*sn't it amazing to watch our young children explore their own bodies? They are in awe, and wonder at its strangeness and beauty. They touch themselves unselfconsciously, familiarizing themselves with every soft curve and hidden opening. They stick their fingers in their ears, curious about where the miniature tunnels lead. They examine each toe, comparing the size and shape. Boys pull on their penis while girls feel the folds in their vagina. With their hands and eyes, our children discover how "wonderfully made" they are.

If I am comfortable with my children's self-exploration, they will know no shame.

Everyone's life is a fairy tale, written by God's fingers.
HANS CHRISTIAN ANDERSEN

How many of us feel our lives have turned out like a fairy tale? Few, no doubt. Yet, if we take a closer look, we may see that our lives contain many of the same themes found in the stories we read to our children. Our princes may not wear shining armor, but our sons, our mates, and our friends do indeed rescue us from time to time. We may even find that we have slayed a few personal dragons. And as for hidden treasures, haven't we unearthed gems at times when life seemed particularly bleak? And didn't we transform back into a loving mother after days of feeling like the wicked witch?

No, there may not always be magic potions to take or wizards who give advice. Yet, somehow as mothers, we manage to concoct our life's tales and they turn out just fine.

I will recognize the magic and adventure in my life. Together, my family and I will create a story worth retelling.

Play

It is a happy talent to know how to play.

RALPH WALDO EMERSON

hildren just know how to play. From the start they interact with the world in a playful manner. Even when they are studying an object, "locking in" on it as if to grasp its meaning, they will erupt into giggles, legs wiggling with delight. Discoveries are cause for playful laughter.

As our child turns four or five, his play becomes more complex. He creates elaborate games with ever-changing rules. He carries on involved conversations with make-believe characters in languages that we can't hope to understand. He needs no props (though a cape never hurts), and he is happy being a super hero or making his shadow across a wall. Through play our child touches upon aspects of life that we often ignore: the absurd, the unusual, the magical, the mystical. What a talented being he is!

My child reminds me that play is essential to well-being.

A child educated only at school is not an educated child.

🚲 GEORGE SANTAYANA

School is a great place to learn. Fortunately, it is not the only great place to learn. At Grandpa's house our child learns about the proper use of tools and how to use a map. At the zoo she learns facts about the amazing mammals and reptiles she's viewing up close. On the beach, she becomes fascinated with the variety of people she sees. We need only open the door to her world, and she will learn.

My child reminds me that learning is an adventure wherever it takes place.

Grief can take care of itself, but to get the full value of joy you must have somebody to divide it with.

☙ MARK TWAIN

*B*efore my grandmother died, my father, my son, and I made the trek to Canada for a long overdue visit. Although she was weak and frail, her eyes brightened when Alexander peeked out from behind my skirt. He quickly got over his shyness and began jumping on the furniture and squealing with delight. Somehow he knew my grandmother would be the perfect audience.

She died the following year, and although I felt terribly sad that she wouldn't have the chance to watch Alexander grow into adulthood, I was deeply grateful for his opportunity to get to know his great-grandmother.

Every now and then something will trigger his memory. "I miss Grammy Dot," he'll say. "Me too," I answer, "but she'll always live in our hearts." And, I suspect, we'll always live in hers, too.

When someone close to us dies, we lose a person we love and a person who has loved us. I will remember that we are all a part of each other.

Choices

The epitome of indecision: having only one tube tied.
🍦 DIANA COPE DUFFY

*M*y friend Diana and I had a good laugh about indecision. She is currently pregnant with her first child, and, although she always thought that would be it, she now finds herself vacillating about the future. "Maybe I'll just have one tube tied," she jokes. "That way, I can *sort* of make a choice about whether to have more children. I'll do my part and let Fate do hers!"

Those of us who have more childbearing years ahead of us understand her dilemma. After our first we can't imagine being able to have enough love or energy for another. Then we have a second. Suddenly our love feels limitless. Our new baby is surprisingly unique, and we want to know what another and another would be like.

Decisions about the future require much soul-searching. I will keep my options open until the answers are clear.

Grandpa: "How long are you planning on nursing him, anyway?"

*T*hose of us who nursed our babies into toddlerhood have faced the inevitable question: "Isn't he getting a little old for that?" Everyone from relatives to neighbors makes comments about a child at the breast. It's as if they suspect our child is forcing us to do something we don't want to do or they fear he'll be asking for "bah-bah" or "ninny" until he graduates from high school.

It takes courage to trust our own choices. It takes courage to do what we feel is best, especially in the face of opposition—and that includes decisions about how long to nurse our child.

Others' feelings about childrearing should not affect my decisions concerning my child's well-being.

Disruption

The drama of birth is over. The cord is cut, the first cry heard: new life has begun. . . . The mother— seeing, hearing, perhaps touching her baby— scarcely notices the world suddenly busying itself around her, let alone how much her body aches. She just participated in a miracle.

🌹 CARROLL DUNHAM

To those who remained at home with Dad or Grandma and Grandpa, our trip to the hospital was disturbing, not miraculous. The little bundle we brought home is intriguing, but it raises many questions. Like why does it cry so much, and why is Mommy so tired all the time? Why does she have to sit on an inflatable donut and feed the baby with her breasts?

Because our children have no concept of what we went through at the hospital, it is even more difficult for them to comprehend the many changes that result. But as we get stronger, the sense of disruption dwindles, and life approaches normal— which, in itself, is a miracle.

We may have to be content with the fact that the miracle of birth is a private one. I will try to share aspects of that miracle with my family.

Now for the first time I had found a daily style of mothering which fitted me, a way of living with this new part of myself which felt right, not perhaps worthy of The Good Housekeeping Seal of Approval, but nonetheless right.

🍦 JANE LAZARRE

*M*any of us are creating new paradigms for mothering simply because we opted to follow our internal dictates instead of those bombarding us from the media. Whether the newest prescriptive was to stay at home or have a career, we defected from the rules. We were "outlaw moms" creating our own style of mothering, one that fit us. The result: a happier, more contented Mom—and kids.

I define my own mothering style. And I will support other mothers as they choose what is best for them.

My husband and I have different parenting styles, but we always agree on one thing: our child's bedtime.

🚲 CONNIE JOHNSON

We're all winding down, the mood in the house is relaxed; we put the chores on hold to attend to our child, bathing him, reading to him, cuddling him. Then right when the world is exactly the way he wants it—we expect him to happily trot off to bed.

"I'm not tired," he cries convincingly. But if we do give in, we're missing a very important point. He needs his rest, and we need to talk to our husband or work on our photo album or watch a movie uninterrupted. We've earned the right to a little adult time, whether our child is tired or not! Tenderly and firmly, we tuck him in, kiss him good night, and assure him we'll be there for him in the morning.

We spend the whole day with our child, the night belongs to us.

God teaches the birds to make nests, yet the nests of all birds are not alike.

🦎 DUWANISH PROVERB

*E*ach of us creates our own "nest." We fashion our home to be a reflection of who we are. We hang pictures on the walls and decorate each room to create an atmosphere that is uniquely personal. Like birds, we build different types of homes to suit our particular tastes. Some of us prefer open space. Others insist on clutter. Some fill the house with antiques and Victorian paintings, while others gravitate toward modern, streamlined simplicity. Whatever its style, our home makes a statement that expresses who we are.

I will take pride in the "nest" I build because it houses those I love.

Who knows the thoughts of a child?

⬧ NORA PERRY

C hildren ask difficult and fascinating questions. While in the changing room at the recreation center they want to know why one woman's breasts are larger than another's. What do we say? Our children ask why the neighbors go to church on Sunday and we don't. They want to know why people are different colors.

Figuring out how to explain the many differences our child observes isn't easy. First we must determine how much she knows *and* how much she's ready to know. Then we have to come up with answers. It's a trial-and-error process. However, if our responses are sincere and respectful, we can trust that our child will have much to ponder, and even more to ask.

My answers are jumping off points for my child's explorations.

Where there is a woman there is magic.

🚲 NTOZAKE SHANGE

hatever magic we offer, our children will remember it fondly. Grandmothers who bake prize-winning cookies without ever consulting a recipe. Aunts who read stories with the bravado of a Shakespearean actor. Big sisters who leap off the high dive, creating their own unique splash in our younger child's life. Mothers who snap their fingers to Motown while preparing spaghetti and meatballs.

Within me resides my own unique magic.

Ever since I was first read to, then started reading to myself, there has never been a line read that I didn't hear. As my eyes followed the sentence, a voice was saying it silently to me. It isn't my mother's voice, or the voice of any person I can identify, certainly not my own. It is human, but inward, and it is inwardly that I listen to it. It is to me the voice of the story or the poem itself.

🌺 EUDORA WELTY

Children love to be read to, and it's no wonder. Their ears hunger for the voice of the story. The characters rise off the page for them, and the thrill of adventure beats deep within their hearts. Eventually he will explore on his own, but for the first few years he depends on us to introduce him to new worlds and the sound and rhythm of words. Reading to our child doesn't have to be restricted to bedtime. Some mothers will read to their toddler while nursing a newborn—and this becomes a special time for everyone.

Children's books can be magical and our child's responses lead us to reimagine the familiar texts and discover the new.

Reading to my child opens him up to new worlds—it is a favorite time of day for both of us.

The secret of dealing successfully with a child is not to be his parent.

🖋 MELL LAZARUS

*B*ecause they never have to play the heavy, our friends can indulge our child to their own, and our child's, delight. We watch in amazement as together they think up games and entertainment that we would never have thought of in a million years. Of course, friends sometimes teach our child things they know we hardly approve of, just to see if we've lost our sense of humor. By the time bedtime rolls around, our kid has a whole new act. He swaggers up to us, and, cool as can be, says: "Hey, baby, what's happenin'." We laugh, egging him on to greater dramatic heights, until there's only one thing left to do—carry him off stage!

Hopefully, after my child goes to sleep, if my friend has any energy left, we adults will have a chance to play and laugh like kids!

Affection never was wasted.

🚲 HENRY WADSWORTH LONGFELLOW

*O*ne of the pleasures of having a five-year-old is watching her take one of those leaps in development. Suddenly, she's pouring her own milk and walking yards ahead of us, and we are struck by her maturity and independence. Then, just as suddenly, she's crawling back into our lap, holding our hand and playing with our hair. She lavishes attention on us, and while we love all the cuddling and the feeling of being "special," it can be overwhelming. We may even fear regressing to the good old days, when we weren't allowed out of her sight. As one mother told me: "Now I remember why I sent her to preschool!"

My five-year-old is capable of great bursts of affection. I will enjoy it while it lasts.

Ask your child what he wants for dinner only if he's buying.

🐻 FRAN LEBOWITZ

*I*t is important to provide our young child with options. It gives him a sense of power and a chance to work on decision-making skills. However, giving him too many options can be overwhelming for him *and* for us. As one mother complained, "I feel like a short-order cook." Her two-and-a-half-year-old is a finicky eater. He's always asking for one thing, then changing his mind, then changing it again. Everything in the pantry ends up on the table, and still her son eats nothing. "He can't live on air," she worries. But like most young children, her son's eating habits are bound to hinge more on growth spurts and need than on Mom's urgings. When he is hungry enough, he'll eat.

So, if we plan to ask our child what he wants for dinner, we'd be smart to limit the selection. Unless, of course, he's buying.

By providing options for my child, I show him that I respect his ability to make choices. Yet I mustn't forget that I compose the menu.

A Child's Logic

All our reasoning ends in surrender to feeling.

🍦 BLAISE PASCAL

ecently Alexander and I flew to Boston to visit my parents. Right after dinner, Alexander enthusiastically shouted, "Grandpa, let's wrestle!" My father, who had not yet finished his meal, turned to Alexander and, in his most serious voice, informed him, "Do you know what will happen if I wrestle right now? In three minutes, I'll throw up." Without missing a beat, Alexander responded, "We'll only wrestle for two minutes." Dad, who has an answer for everything, was speechless. Ten minutes later, with all of us on Alexander's side, my father had no choice but to yield to his grandson's power of reasoning. Their wrestling match was the highlight of the evening.

It's wonderful to witness my child's growing ability to reason. And often equally wonderful to watch those on the receiving end.

We parents sometimes feel that the interruptions, hassles, and inconveniences of parenting are standing in the way of our growth. We don't realize, however, that the constant change and adjustment are teaching us every moment. They propel us forward . . . bringing forth our true greatness. As we endeavor to teach our children, they are the ones who are truly teaching us.

                              JOYCE AND BARRY VISSELL

*W*hat makes parenting so challenging? The learning never seems to stop. At first we may feel that our children stand in the way of our growth. Certainly their constant interruptions can slow down our projects. However, it is our children who "propel us forward" by demanding more of us than we would have ever demanded of ourselves.

With children, we are forced to focus so we use time more wisely. In addition, we are constantly confronted with who we are, and that presents us with opportunities to change and grow.

My child is my teacher. Under his tutelage I can look forward to becoming a wiser me.

Outnumbered

They were becoming like a little Mafia. If one committed a mischief, the others would not tell.

🏛 FRANCO DILIGENTI

With our third child, we are outnumbered and the little imps quickly learn to gang up on us. Their specialty? Figuring out what Mom and Dad *least* agree on. They pit us against each other, and while we're deep in discussion, they commit their mischief. We stumble on the evidence everywhere, crunching on the dry pasta spilled all over the kitchen floor, or discovering super heroes swimming in the toilet bowl. We parents unite, but when we line them up for interrogation, they try to look their most angelic. If they see we're not buying it, they may resort to desperate measures—even blaming the dog!

My kids stick together. If my husband and I know what's good for us, we will too.

Animals are such agreeable friends—they ask no questions, they pass no criticisms.

GEORGE ELIOT

hildren love pets. At least, they love the idea of having a pet. When reality sets in, however, visions of a cuddly puppy that's as docile as a stuffed bear can quickly fade. When we hug the newest member of our family, our children struggle to climb into our lap to claim their share of attention. When we let the puppy lick our face, they complain, obviously jealous of "the little guy."

As time passes, our child will develop a relationship with the family pet and will embrace him as a friend and companion.

As my child and I together care for our pet, he will become "one of the gang."

To respect that fury or those giddy high spirits or a body that seems perpetually mobile is respecting nature, much as one respects the strength of a hurricane, the rush of a waterfall.

🚲 SARA RUDDICK

Some of us have spirited children, children with inexhaustable energy. They bounce around the house with irrepressible exuberance. Their wills are strong and they take life head-on, both physically and mentally. We can't keep anything out of their reach—there isn't a barrier that they won't attempt to climb. And we can't keep secrets from them, either. They'll ask question after question until their curiosity is appeased.

We respect their spirited nature. We are in awe of their energy. Lovingly, we will help our child direct this energy toward productive ends.

If I help my child focus his spirited nature, I can later watch him move mountains.

*Celebrate the silence. It is your given name. And
what you remember of your own full moonlight.*

🐾 COOPER EDENS

*O*ur need for meditative silence is often the
most neglected of our needs. We try to
find the time, but there is none. We try to make
time, and unexpected events disrupt our retreat.
Yet, we must trust that within us is a place where
we live
all alone. It's where we go to renew ourselves,
where we go to get in touch with the purpose of
our life: why we chose to have children; why we
pursued a particular career; why we married the
person we did.

Eventually, the opportunity for such meditation
will be more abundant. But in the meantime we
must grab every opportunity for a brief visit. When
we find ourselves straightening up a room or sitting in freeway traffic, we might take a deep
breath and open up to where our real self lives.

**My silence resides within. Lest I forget the way, I
must go there regularly.**

*Sing, sweetness, to the last palpitation of the evening
and the breeze.*

ST. JOHN PERSE

*T*he days are long and the livin' is easy. Maybe for everyone else. For us it means later bedtimes, earlier mornings, and fewer organized activities to fill the gap. But it is nice spending more time with our child. We swim together, work in the garden, take a trip or two. Memories of our own summers return—smells of charcoal and chlorine and freshly cut grass, the feel of seersucker pajamas on sunburned shoulders, the freedom of playing on and on until dark—and the rhythm of life relaxes.

Then along about mid-August, the first school notice arrives. Alarm clocks and school lunches and strict bedtimes are just around the corner. Eventually, the family will readjust to the routines ahead, but until then, let's raise a glass of lemonade and toast the last moments of summer bliss.

My family will have to adjust and readjust to new routines. If I remain flexible, I can keep us on track and enjoy the flow.

Body Wisdom

The body has its own way of knowing, a knowing that has little to do with logic, and much to do with truth, little to do with control, and much to do with acceptance . . .

                     MARILYN SEWELL

The body "knows." It "speaks" through gestures and movements, through expressions and sound, but we rarely listen. Instead, we focus on ways to "improve" it, to make it more attractive—ways to alter it externally to fit the current images of beauty and style.

For many of us, the dramatic changes of pregnancy forced us to be aware of our body for the first time. And we listened to and followed its internal dictates. Now that our body has returned to "normal," it is up to us to maintain contact with its deeper wisdom.

If I stay in tune with my body's internal wisdom, health and beauty will be its external expression.

Englishwomen dress as if they had been a mouse in a previous incarnation, or hope to be in the next.

🐭 DAME EDITH SITWELL

*A*nd so do mothers . . . Weary from extracting stain after stain from our better clothes, we tend to start dressing down. Casual clothes are more appropriate to life with small children, but after a while, a wardrobe of blue jeans and sweatpants can become tiresome. Our shapeless clothes begin to match our self-image, and we feel unattractive and plain.

Thankfully, with our child's growing autonomy, we can begin to incorporate more flattering fashions. If we have a waist left, we belt it, reclaiming the sensuality of our curves. Perhaps we choose a new hairstyle and purchase an outfit that enhances our femininity. And while clothes don't "make the woman," they can help us to reassert a positive self-image.

Updating my wardrobe can help me to express a more varied and complete self-image.

When elephants fight it is the grass that suffers.

AFRICAN SAYING

*A*s mothers, we often suppress our anger toward our partner for fear of frightening our child with heated arguments. Yet, to pretend that we always get along with our partner distorts reality. While we must be careful to shield our child from unnecessary and explosive conflicts, it is important for him to know that even a close and loving relationship experiences anger and tears. By the same token, we need to share the resolution of our anger with our child. Otherwise, all he experiences is "elephants fighting," and he suffers.

I want my child to understand that anger—and resolution—is a normal part of every relationship.

Like all cultures, one of the family's first jobs is to persuade its members they're special, more wonderful than the neighboring barbarians. The persuasion consists of stories showing family members demonstrating admirable traits, which it claims are family traits. Attention to the stories' actual truth is never the family's most compelling consideration. Encouraging the belief is. The family's survival depends on the shared sensibility of its members.

                                  ELIZABETH STONE

Some of us come from families that encourage, even demand, exclusivity. Anyone who marries into the family is still treated as an outsider. Under the guise of "family loyalty," feelings are hurt and hearts are broken as family members are forced to choose between our partner and the clan.

As parents, we can take a different approach, teaching our children the value of accepting others. And we can create a larger circle of support from "chosen family"—special friends who love us without exacting a price.

Families can segregate, families can unite. I choose to make family an inclusive force in my child's life.

It is a good answer that knows when to stop.

🦋 ITALIAN PROVERB

*Y*oung children ask about *everything*. They find our tampons, and pretending the applicator is a cigar, they ask: "What's this?" When we try to be vague and reply: "It belongs to Mommy," they become even more curious. "I mean, what is it *for*?" they press. Seeing the perplexed look on our face, they're now completely intrigued. Should we try to answer with simple biological facts that they can understand, or should we save ourselves the embarrassment and lie? Surely they wouldn't know whether that strange thing they found in our drawer this morning is a diaphragm or, as my friend Liz offered, "a bathing cap for the cat!"

My young child puts my wits to the test. I think she has more questions than I have answers.

*Taunting is just a way of messing with language,
seeing what it can do, testing it, in its most extreme
form, to see if it has any power.*

🍦 BRUCE BROOKS

*A*n annoying fact of raising young children is
that they soon learn the power of words—
especially ones they know are taboo. "Jellyfish,"
"Butthead," and "Barnaclebrain" can pepper their
speech with alarming frequency. "Could be worse,"
we think. And once our child starts playing with the
older kids in the park, we discover that it *is* worse.

We are assigned the unpleasant duty of eradicat-
ing certain words from our child's vocabulary without overreacting to them. At first we try ignoring the
words, knowing that if we act shocked, their power
increases. Then we encourage him to use more
acceptable words to express his feelings, and we
reward him with a hug when he does.

**Using naughty words is my child's way of
experimenting with power. I must use my
words to communicate what is appropriate
and what is not.**

Women as the guardians of children possess great power. They are the molders of their children's personalities and the arbiters of their development.

ANN OAKLEY

*A*ll mothers have the urge to "take charge." As primary caregivers, we may have more vested in directing our child. After all, we know her best. Yet, if we can manage to stand back and observe others who care for her, we may learn a great deal. For example, she uses a naughty word in front of the baby-sitter, and instead of giving her the usual time-out, she tells her, "I don't like that word. It hurts my feelings." Our child, we notice, refrains from further use. It was not the way we would have dealt with the situation, but it was effective. We all benefitted from a fresh approach.

It is important to remember that many styles of relating and disciplining are good for my child—and *me*.

The Eskimos had fifty-two names for snow because it was important to them: there ought to be as many for love.

🐾 MARGARET ATWOOD

oddlers often try to figure out the many distinctions that apply to adult life. "How come Mommy loves Daddy in a different way than she loves Uncle Brian?" they wonder. "Can Mommy love me *and* my baby sister the same amount?" And, "Why do I love Mommy more than anyone else?" they question out loud. That is when we find ourselves explaining the many different kinds of love that exist. Wouldn't it be easier if we had many more words for love? After all, what is more varied and important to us?

I will show my child that there are many faces of love.

Candor

Childhood candor . . . shall I ever find you again.

LEO TOLSTOY

*C*hildren will use the most elemental terms when talking about the people they meet. "I want to play with the brown girl across the street," they say if they haven't yet learned her name. "There's a new Jewish boy in my class," they announce, returning home from school. While such comments may sound racist to our ears, we need to realize that our children are not making judgments, their comments are usually descriptive. It is only when they pick up and voice negative connotations to these words, that we need to address the very adult invention of prejudice.

It's important to remember that my child's description of the people he meets is exactly that—*description*, not judgment.

The greatest strength is gentleness.

🚲 IROQUOIS PROVERB

Setting limits for young children usually requires a firm stance. The more that stance is challenged, the firmer we get. After several ignored pronouncements, we're apt to start counting. We get to three, maybe five. Soon we're threatening punishments, and then we're reduced to shouting. What we've done is confuse "firm" with "harsh." We've forgotten that gentleness can be our greatest strength.

When we remember to use discipline as a teaching tool, we are less likely to approach situations with "an iron-hand" and more likely to respond through our resources of inner strength.

Some may see gentleness as "giving in," but I see it as setting limits with love, not anger.

Cooperation is doing with a smile what you have to do anyway.

🕊 ANONYMOUS

A positive attitude can mean the difference between enjoying each task and feeling oppressed by it. We expend so much energy finding ways around washing the dishes, or resenting doing the laundry and paying the bills, but when we approach these tasks with a smile, chores can begin to seem more like accomplishments. Cooperating with life's obligations in the same way we ask our children to cooperate with us, allows a momentum to build. And soon we find ourselves moving smoothly through the day, not fighting against it.

When I cooperate with life, I enjoy it more. I may still have too much to do, but I am in sync with the flow.

*Each friend represents a world in us, a world possibly
not born until they arrive, and it is only by this meeting that a new world is born.*

> ANAIS NIN

Remember the sadness of losing our first
best friend? It was so inexplicable, yet so
final. Now we see it happening to our toddler. Suddenly, he and his best friend are finding it hard to
relate. His friend wants to build towers and play
castle while our son wants only to climb trees or
wrestle, and their play dates end in frustration.
We're reluctant to interfere, yet we long to smooth
things over.

So, we talk to our child about the nature of relationships. We help him find other friends who love
the backyard as much as he does. And we encourage him to try his hand at castle-building. He may
not only develop a new skill but a new way to
relate to an old friend.

**My child is experiencing the ebb and flow of
friendship. I will help him understand that no
one person can fulfill all his needs.**

Analysis consists in saying a truth only when the other person is ready for it, has been prepared for it by an organic process of gradation and evolution.

☙ ANAIS NIN

We're hardly over the hump of our infant's "stranger anxiety" when we have to start confronting our own. We don't want to frighten our child. Yet, like it or not, we must prepare her for unpleasant everyday realities, and we may need to inform her before she's fully able to process it. There are storybooks that talk about strangers in ways that young children can understand. And there are some basic rules, for example, about what to do if our child gets separated from us. Then, as she becomes more mature, we can elaborate on basic information, giving her specific rules to apply to a variety of situations.

When my child's safety becomes an issue for me, it is an issue for her, as well. If I prepare her properly, both of us will sleep better at night.

*I started painting as a hobby. My husband was very
supportive until I started doing exhibits away from
home. When I returned, after only being away for a
few days, my husband would reprimand me.*

🌺 ANONYMOUS MOTHER

*B*ecoming successful at work can create a
backlash at home. Our husband says he's
proud of us, but one night leaving a dinner party,
we catch him thanking our hosts for "the first home-
cooked meal we've had in weeks." Or, finding no
milk for his coffee, he explodes, "Doesn't *anyone*
ever go shopping anymore?" Anyone, meaning us.

Whether our husband resents our success or is
just frightened of change, he is sending double
messages. And we need to speak up and clear
the air.

**I resent having to choose between my marriage
and work. Perhaps if I learn to express my
feelings, I won't have to.**

Discouragement is simply the despair of wounded self-love.

☞ FRANCOIS DE FENELON

*E*ver notice how, when we aren't feeling good about ourselves, we tend to discourage our children from taking chances? We become tentative, afraid to allow our children to take risks because we know too well the frustration and self-doubt that comes from failing. We think we're protecting them, but when we discourage our children from taking chances, so much learning is lost.

We know we will love our children whether or not they succeed. If we love ourselves in the same unconditional way, we will not fear failure and will dare to take full advantage of life's offerings.

Self-love is the key to being able to take risks. I will set an example for my child.

The best antidepressants are expression and action. That way our depression is not an end but a meaningful beginning.

🚲 MARILYN FERGUSON

We all experience occasional depression, times when our energy is low and we feel blue. Sometimes our depression can be blamed on exhaustion. At other times, more deep-seated causes are at issue. Although it is tempting to force ourselves to be "up," it is important to "sit with" our feelings long enough to understand them. Only then are we capable of taking the necessary action to change a situation from bad to good.

Maybe we need a talk with a close friend. Maybe we need to ask our baby-sitter for more hours. Perhaps we need to stand up for ourselves at work. Expressing our feelings and taking action is empowering. It's a meaningful start to creating a more permanent change in our life.

Depression has many causes *and* cures. Once I understand it, I will know what action to take to chase away the blues.

. . . I never realized before that a letter—a mere sheet of paper—could be such a spiritual thing—could emanate so much feeling—you gave a soul to it!

TINA MODOTTI

A letter from a friend is a gift of enormous proportion. In our hands, at our fingertips, are the details of her life; the thoughts so carefully written down for our eyes only. We laugh with her, cry with her, and best yet, embark on a conversation that can be replayed anytime we need to escape.

We steal the time to respond. We sit quietly and pensively and pass along our unspoken thoughts and comments on our day. It is the best thanks we can give.

A letter from a cherished friend is a heartfelt gift, a message from the soul.

There's often a big temptation for persons on the spiritual way to leave their ordinary life behind and seek a greater involvement in "practice." But they have to realize that our practice is always done right where we are.

🍦 JOAN RIECK

*F*ew of us have the luxury of leaving our lives behind and devoting ourselves totally to spiritual practice. Although we may feel that such singular focus is beyond us, we can discover what Zen masters have always known: Begin where you are. Even the chaos of our daily lives can be the "stuff" that illuminates the soul. Just think of it. What better way to learn patience and perseverance than being a mother? We cannot simply give up when the lessons get too rigorous. Instead, we must learn to find peace in the midst of swirling food fights, discipline in the midst of rebellion, and compassion in the midst of criticism. What better way to learn about love?

Mothers don't need to leave home to be "on the path." I can practice right where I am.

If you harbor ill will toward your parents, you have disowned part of yourself.

🚲 ADELAIDE BRY

*M*ost of us wind up following different paths than our parents took, but some of us take that path out of anger toward them. We may overcompensate with our own children, pushing them in areas where we found no encouragement and holding back in areas where we felt smothered. We must question and challenge the behavior of our parents, but until we come to terms with their foibles, we will continue to live our lives as a reaction to them.

Recognizing the qualities—both good and bad—that I've inherited from my parents helps me to forgive them, and move on.

*Spiritual energy brings compassion into the world.
With compassion, we see benevolently our own
human condition and the condition of our own
fellow beings. We drop prejudice. We withhold
judgment.*

🌹 CHRISTINA BALDWIN

We can tell when spiritual energy has perme-
ated our existence, not because it is so
joyful, but because it is authentic. It moves us to
tears and to laughter. It makes us feel loved and
loving.

Our young child fills us with such Spirit, and the
compassion we feel for him extends out into the
world—to the abused child down the block, to our
lonely widowed neighbor, to the alcoholic who just
sneered at our little girl.

**My child opens my heart; the rest of the world is
the beneficiary.**

I remember when I was very young and I saw the circus. I thought: "How can life be like that? Can you live that way and always pay attention to the absurd?"

🍦 PAT OLESZKO

*W*atching a child's sense of humor evolve is an amazing thing. At first, dry wit and off-the-wall jokes go right over his head. Slapstick silliness seems to be the only sure hit. Yet, as our child grows, so does his sense of subtety. He begins to understand shades of humor. Sarcasm, which used to go right over his head, is now coming out of his mouth. Living with a smart aleck can be trying, but we can't deny the fact that our child comes up with some "good ones." We laugh until we're weak. And for weeks, just the mention of that moment sends us both off into gales of laughter.

I can depend on my child's spontaneous antics to keep me laughing.

Parents are strange for their age.

              🚲 AMANDA VAIL

*I*f we think children do strange things, just think how we must look to them. Odd creatures, at best. When we rush around, consulting our watch every five minutes to make sure we're not late, kids think we're nuts. What (short of ice cream or balloons) could possibly be so important? We put makeup on our face. Our children think, "Okay, that's neat," and then we ruin it all by willingly choosing asparagus over french fries. I guess it depends on how you look at it. From their point of view, or ours.

From my child's perspective, I may make some pretty strange choices, too.

Laugh not to scorne (neither) olde ne young, Be of good bering and have a good tongue.

🌸 A NORTHERN MOTHER

*T*eaching our young children to say "please" and "thank you" is an unavoidable part of mothering, especially for those of us who don't enjoy being treated like a slave. Yet, are we sometimes too quick with our reminders to "use your magic words"? Are we taking away our children's initiative to be polite? Aren't there times when a respectful tone of voice is enough? The answer is probably yes, thank you.

The more I use *my* magic words, the less I may find myself having to ask for them.

Sibling Rivalry

It goes without saying that you should never have more children than you have car windows.

🍦 ERMA BOMBECK

Siblings can argue over the seating arrangement in a car, the color of their toothbrushes, or the amount of food on their plates. Why? Because children are born with an innate sense of entitlement, and they regard as their birthright all of our undivided attention and love. So when there are more than one of them, they're bound to be rivals.

Although it's useless to think we can end sibling rivalry altogether, there are some creative ways around it. One mother of four assigned ownership to any object—toy, book, or clothing—that entered the house. No one was expected to share what was his, but no one could expect others to share either. Soon all were bartering and sharing without even knowing it. To end bickering over who got "more," another mother would give one daughter the honor of cutting a brownie in half and the other the bonus of picking her piece first.

Siblings were made to rival. Moms were made to make sure things don't unravel.

Imagination is more important than knowledge.

🚲 ALBERT EINSTEIN

Three-year-old: "Do Ninja Turtles have penises?"

Nine-year-old: "I don't think they do."

Three-year-old: "Then how do they go pee-pee?"

Aren't we lucky to be privy to such conversations? Not only do we have a good laugh, but we get a chance to see how our child's mind works, how he reasons things out for himself.

No longer is he satisfied with just any old answer. In fact, he keeps questioning until the answer fits his view of the world and makes sense to his forming intellect.

I don't want my child to accept all the "answers" he is given. The questions he asks and the conclusions he draws often make me smile.

If we wonder often, the gift of knowledge will come.

ARAPAHO PROVERB

Young children are full of questions, good questions that require thought and knowledge about a variety of topics. Sometimes, though, our elaborate explanations are more than they can use. If we don't know when to stop, we need only pay attention to when our child tunes out. A good answer stimulates our child to open new doors, not to shut us out.

If I want my child to keep asking questions, my answers will be short and to the point.

We look and see the goodness in other people, but we don't see it in ourselves. The act of turning around and catching the goodness in ourselves is to wake up. Our consciousness, that lost, scared soldier, finally meets itself.

NATALIE GOLDBERG

Children are born with self-love. It is up to us to keep this love alive. Part of how we do this is by applauding their accomplishments, instilling self-confidence and pride. But even more importantly, we let them know that we love them for who they are, just as they are.

I want my children to always love themselves. I will teach them to see their goodness.

It seemed as if I had lived many lives, that I had turned to smoke each night, and been reborn each morning.

🚲 ISABEL ALLENDE

Sometimes we feel as though we always wake up the same old self living the same old routine. The unrelenting constantness of motherhood makes us feel that things will never change. Trying to keep a stiff upper lip, we fulfill our duties, but silently we long for change.

Then, like a swift yet subtle brush stroke that alters an entire painting, our lives do change. It need not be anything of major significance and it may not be an external change, but something shifts inside us. A new perspective emerges, an aspect of ourselves blossoms, and each morning we feel reborn.

There are phases in my life of accelerated internal change. I will celebrate these new passages of growth.

*You spend your life doing something they put people
in asylums for.*

🎗 JANE FONDA

*M*s. Fonda was referring to acting, yet her
words could as easily apply to mother-
hood. Like how we start talking to ourselves, narrat-
ing the course of our day, or holding conversations
with inanimate objects just to confirm that we're still
capable of entertaining adult thoughts.

Then there are those times when we pretend to
be someone else—Traffic Cop, Wonder Woman,
Madonna—to amuse our child. There's no telling
what we'll invent, especially if a bout of chicken
pox has kept us all quarantined for awhile. Occasionally our make-believe gets so wacky and wild
that our children look at us as if we've finally lost
our minds.

**When I apply basic acting techniques to
mothering, there's no telling what (or who)
will emerge!**

Noise

For children is there any happiness which is not also noise?

🍦 FREDERICK W. FABER

Children love to make noise. Their play is so boisterous and exuberant that it's impossible to suppress the variety and volume of sounds. As those of us with young children know, the older they get, the more noise fills the house: laughter, arguments, squeals of delight. Now it isn't only our child's noise, but hers plus two or three of her friends who have joined in the merriment. And it seems as if the more noise they make, the happier they are.

While we're pleased to see our children having such a grand time, what a relief to hear the silence when the noise stops.

I enjoy the sounds of children and feel they are a part of me, just as the silence is part of me.

*Somewhere in our lives, each of us needs a free place,
a little psychic territory. Do you have yours?*

GLORIA STEINEM

*L*ike us, our toddler needs a place where she
can be alone. It may be a place to play with
her toys without having to share them with her little
sister. It may be a place to shed the burdensome
responsibilities of being the oldest. She may even
ask for a room of her own. Yet, as she quickly discovers, independence has its price. She may feel
lonely in her new room and even miss the company
of her grabby baby sister. So what happens? She
spends most of her time in the younger one's room.
Until the baby starts pestering her again, that is.

**Like me, my child is learning how to balance
social interaction with solitude. And, like me, she
will come to value both.**

Making terms with reality, with things as they are, is a full-time business for the child.

🎖 MILTON R. SAPIRSTEIN

By the time our child reaches age four or five his desire to compete is evident. Suddenly, he must always be first at everything. "I get the first cookie!" he commands. "First one in the house!" he shouts racing ahead of everyone. The desire to be first may be particularly strong if our child spends a lot of time with older siblings or neighborhood kids. When the "big kids" race to the end of the block, our young one follows and quickly discovers how frustrating competition can be.

It's time to introduce the concept of "doing one's best." At first it may be difficult for our child to understand why the "big kids" always outrun or outjump him. But if he also spends time at activities he and his peers can handle, he will discover that everybody excels at something. As one child exclaimed, "I'm the best at crawling through tight spots because I'm the smallest!"

Teaching my child to value his own strengths can lessen his need to be first all the time.

*Permissiveness is the principle of treating children as
if they were adults; and the tactic of making sure
they never reach that stage.*

🍦THOMAS SZASZ

*I*t is tempting to treat our young children like
miniature adults. Verbally, they sound like
adults, offering opinions and information on a variety of subjects. Sometimes they act as though they
know exactly what they're talking about. But *we*
know better, and it's important to remember that
while they may have an intellectual grasp of things,
they may not have the emotional maturity to know
what is best for them. For this reason, we need to
resist the temptation of giving them more responsibility than they can handle, and to remind ourselves
that it takes years of guidance to teach them to
determine what is appropriate and in their best
interest.

**When I permit my children to make adult
choices, I am doing them a disservice. After
all, *I* am the adult.**

The Phone

Every time I pick up the phone, I'm suddenly irresistible.

ANONYMOUS MOTHER

Whether we're housebound or officebound, few of us have time for anything but over-the-wire meetings with friends. And maybe it's because our phone conversations are so precious that they become such kid-magnets.

We try to time it just right, but no matter how entrenched he may be in Leggo land, the minute we pick up the telephone, his antennae go up. Suddenly his blocks won't fit together, or he needs help on the potty, or he can't wait another minute for a hug and kiss. If we're afraid of discouraging his displays of affection, it helps to remember that there's someone hanging on the other end, and she's probably rolling her eyes.

It's up to me to decide when my child genuinely needs my attention and when he must learn to wait his turn.

Give and Take

If you want to be listened to, you should put in time listening.

🐞 MARGE PIERCY

*D*uring a recent visit, I watched my son make various advances toward members of my family, only to be ignored. His four-year-old attempts to get their attention were often treated as no more than background noise. The seen-and-not-heard adage apparently was a mainstay of the household. On the other hand, he was expected to be receptive to anything coming his way. Because they were adults, my relatives expected instantaneous response, no questions asked.

Interestingly enough, when Alexander hadn't warmed up to them after several days of such one-sidedness, they were baffled. I couldn't admit it, but I was proud. My son understands that no relationship is a given. Even when it comes to family.

Children know when people are truly interested in them and when they are only pretending. Wouldn't we do well to follow their example?

People can expect to get back what they give—especially when it comes to children.

Even without wars, life is dangerous.

🍦 ANNE SEXTON

We know too well the feeling of being outnumbered. Our neighbors come to pick up their child after a playdate and decide to stay for dinner. Relatives pay us an unannounced visit. The television is blaring; the couch has been turned into a trampoline; and no one seems to be listening to a word we say. We look at our watch, but no one makes a move. "Excuse me," we say loudly, "its time for Michael to go to bed." "Oh, he can stay up just a few more minutes," says Aunt Margaret, who won't be around in the morning to deal with him.

We try to remain casual, cheerful, and polite, but all we want to do is scream, "Everybody out!" It's time to bring in our second line of defense: Dad. He reminds us that we are not crazy, and together we bring the noise level down, escort the guests to the door, and lead our child off to bed.

My husband and I need to be a solid team, especially when we're outnumbered!

Nothing is more sad than the death of an illusion.

ARTHUR KOESTLER

hether we are aware of it or not, we all enter into motherhood with preconceived notions about the kind of mother we will be. Then, when our child is born, reality sets in. We don't always look our best. The house isn't always clean. We don't have the energy to entertain our relatives during every holiday season.

But illusions die hard, especially where motherhood is concerned. We seem convinced that there are these "perfect mothers" out there (though we haven't met any), and we feel bad about falling short of our ideal image. What we need to do is give our illusions a proper burial. Like a New Orleans funeral—with plenty of pomp and brass—we can let them die and celebrate our own style of mothering.

My illusions can get in the way of being myself. Instead of mourning their demise, I choose to rejoice in the freedom of letting them go.

If there were no schools to take the children away from home part of the time, the insane asylums would be filled with mothers.

E.W. HOWE

I once heard a mother say: "No one person should be with a child for more than four hours at a time." Though I didn't understand it then, now that I have a child, I know exactly what she meant. There is no experience more intense than child rearing. It takes all our energy and focus, discipline and creativity. Meryl Streep said it well: "To be a really good mother you have to be an extraordinary woman. You have to keep yourself involved with your children during great periods of the day when it's just the two of you and you feel that at any moment you may literally go out of your mind."

I am grateful for all those who contribute their time and energy to my child, especially when I need a break from the intensity.

Friends are a second existence.

🍦 BALTASAR GRACIAN

*W*e all have single friends. We look at the freedom they have and can't help but feel a twinge of jealousy. Their lives appear to be so carefree, and we can see there's nothing "spare" about their spare time. They're taking trips around the world; we're going to Disneyland. They're sipping café au lait in bed on Sunday mornings; we're trying to pretend we're asleep while tiny creatures bounce around our head.

It might surprise us to hear that they find our lives enviable. They ask to "borrow" our child for the afternoon, just for the company. And as chaotic as our dinners together may be, our friends draw comfort from the spirit of family they feel in our home.

If I share my kids with my single friends, maybe they'll share their frequent flier tickets with me!

I believe that the child should be taught from the very first that the whole world is his world, that adult and child share one world, that all generations are needed.

🚲 PEARL S. BUCK

I was fortunate to grow up in a richly diverse neighborhood. I had playmates of many different races, religions, and ages. It seemed that in every household there were grandmothers who embraced me as their own. My friends and I ate their cookies and climbed up into their laps to listen to their stories. We learned native songs and dances and joined in holiday celebrations that were nothing like our own. The neighborhood brought us together and taught us that different does not necessarily mean strange.

How sad that our elders are so much less present in our children's lives, that our communities and schools are so homogenized, and that we are often too busy to notice the imbalance.

I want my child to grow up with the knowledge that all peoples and all generations contribute to the richness of life.

Being a mother means that I must be available to my children, not all the time, mind you, but enough so they know I am receptive to whatever they have to share. This is the basis of good communication.

🌷 BETH SHANNON

Some of us have come to think that being a mother means that we must drop whatever we're doing whenever our child thinks he needs our attention. But if we try to be available all the time, we may find ourselves focusing only on our child's needs. When we establish a climate of inclusiveness, an "open door" that swings both ways, we give our child the security of knowing that his needs will be fulfilled along with the needs of others. He will know that he will not have to fight for attention when something's important to him; and, by the same token, we will not have to fight for those moments of uninterrupted calm we so desperately need.

A part of me is always on call to answer my child's needs. I will reserve the rest of me for myself.

"Use Your Words"

Words are a form of action, capable of influencing change. Their articulation represents a complete, lived experience.

🖋 INGRID BENGIS

his simple advice—"use your words"— becomes a mother's mantra. With it, we encourage our children to use brains rather than brawn when settling disputes. Yet, do our children really understand what we mean? Not right away. That's why we must keep repeating these words.

Even when they don't seem to be sinking in, we persist, as in the case of the mother who began listening in on an argument between her daughters. When the confrontation looked as if it might get out of hand, the mother stepped in and insisted, "use your words." Without skipping a beat, the youngest said to her sister, "Briana may I *please* kick you?"

Over and over, I will demonstrate the benefit of using words so that my child will eventually understand their power.

The more people have studied different methods of bringing up children, the more they have come to the conclusion that what good mothers and fathers instinctively feel like doing for their babies is the best after all.

🚲 BENJAMIN SPOCK

*I*t takes us first-time mothers a while to trust our instincts. All the competing parenting theories can overwhelm and confuse us to the point that we have difficulty determining what we feel is best for our child. Through much trial and error we learn to trust our natural abilities. We come to know what will work and what won't.

We have our second child, and in many ways it's like starting from scratch. This baby looks, acts, and feels entirely different from our first. However, because we are more secure in our mothering techniques, we will be more confident and self-assured, knowing instinctively when to dismiss theories that do not apply to our child.

My first child taught me to rely on instinct. My second child will benefit from the confidence I have in my mothering.

Traveling

In America there are two classes of travel—first-class, and with children.

🕊️ROBERT CHARLES BENCHLEY

When we were new mothers, even the mention of the word "travel" filled us with dread. But now our toddler seems ready and eager to hit the road. Being big enough to actually see out the window helps turn car trips into adventures. Trains are fascinating. And airplanes are especially magical.

Wearing his pilot's wings, our child feels grown-up. He's proud to carry his own flight bag, which we've filled with surprises. He's so intrigued by the way the food's packaged we don't even care that he doesn't eat a bite. And together, we are awed by the tiny cars moving far below and amazed to be passing through the clouds.

My child is no longer a traveling terror but a fellow adventurer.

Family Reunions

The events of childhood do not pass, but repeat themselves like seasons of the year.

🍦 ELEANOR FARJEON

Children draw families together. They give us all an excuse to gather for holidays and weekends. We return "home" with our young ones, changed, and with a new sense of the importance of connection. Family reunions not only become more important, they become more fun. We discover the essential and enduring quality of family ties, and how comforting it feels to be part of a big, noisy whole. We realize how much we want our children to know their cousins, and we remember the friends we had in our cousins. We *make* time to visit and renew these connections.

My children reconnect me with my family in a special way, renewing and strengthening the bonds of love and shared experience.

You cannot write for children . . . They're much too complicated. You can only write books that are of interest to them.

🚲 MAURICE SENDAK

Children are complex. Although reading about general characteristics and developmental phases can be helpful, each child remains stubbornly unique. Almost at birth, our infant begins showing strong preferences for certain objects and people. By the time she reaches age four, she's a strange little package of biases, preferences, and temperament. Although genetics and environment can explain a great deal, we must stay wary of tidy definitions. No matter how hard we try to figure out our child, much mystery remains.

Getting to know my child is a lifelong process. I look forward to growing up with her.

It's easier to take care of a classroom full of kids than two of my own.

🌺 CLAIRE "TEACHER CLAIRE" KOUKOUTSAKIS

*I*sn't it amazing to see how well-behaved our children act when they're with other people? They readily use "please" and "thank you" without being prompted. They share ice cream and prized possessions. Exercising a self-discipline we rarely witness, they offer to be helpful, cleaning up messes before their departure. We can be proud that, while in public, at least, they know how to behave. Isn't it wonderful to see our "little angels' at their best?

Though they may not always show it at home, my children have internalized much of the discipline I've been trying to instill.

When does a woman stop having children?

🍦 LINDA D'AGROSA

*M*y dear friend Linda posed this question to me when I went to visit her in St. Louis. And I could tell she had already given it a great deal of thought.

Like many of us, Linda loved children long before she started having them. There is nothing in the world she cares for more deeply than her family, and her desire for a large family is strong. But each decision to have another child has presented her with a quandry. On the one hand there are her personal needs and desires; on the other, a list of social concerns ranging from overpopulation and diminishing natural resources to financial constraints.

Three children later, Linda is still making up her mind. In the end, I trust her to make the decision that is right for her *and* the world.

My children—like my job and my community service—are my contributions to the world. Only I can know when my family is complete.

Consistency

Does it seem impossible that the child will grow up? That the bashful smile will become a bold expression . . . that a briefcase will replace the blue security blanket?

ANN BEATTIE

hen our child is born, it is difficult to imagine him being anything but a baby. Yet, by the time he's three years old, we realize that he's anything but a baby. He has his own thoughts, his own imaginings and ways of seeing the world. He has his own opinions about how things should be done. If we skip a word in a favorite story, he'll point it out. If we fail to fill his cereal bowl with the right amount of flakes, he asserts himself with commanding authority.

While our toddler may at times seem overbearing, we must remember how much effort it takes simply to adjust to a constantly changing environment that he has so little control over. It's helpful to remember that the consistency and order we provide will help our child outgrow this three-year-old behavior.

My baby is growing up. I must not minimize what a formidable task that can be—for us both.

Development of character consists solely in moving toward self-sufficiency.

🐾 QUENTIN CRISP

Self-sufficiency is very important to our young child. She can't wait to be able to do all those grown-up things, like using the scissors, casting with Dad's fishing rod, or turning the steering wheel of the car. Yet, isn't it funny to watch her regress when a younger sibling suddenly grows attached to one of her "baby things": an old high chair or rattle or a small quilt embroidered with lambs. With ferocious intensity, she demands it back. Or, at the very least, she refuses to let little brother or sister have it. Forgetting for the moment how hard she is trying to grow up, she'd much prefer that we store it as a keepsake to pay homage to her infancy.

My toddler's attachment to "baby things" is an important link to her past. I will respect her need to hold onto memories.

Dreams

It is the vast, formless, unknown and unknowable things we fear. Anything which can be brought to a common point—a focus within our understanding—can be dealt with.

🍦 LARA JEFFERSON

*I*t isn't unusual to be awakened at night by our child's dreams. "It's mine! It's mine!" we hear him calling out. A few months later, we hear words that sound like encounters with monsters and "bad guys," or replays of unresolved arguments with an older sibling. While occasionally disturbing, these dreams serve as valuable indicators of growth. What we hear at night can help us to be more sensitive to the challenges our child faces during the day.

When I listen to my child's dreams, I begin to understand his daytime monsters and am better able to assist him.

If a child lives with approval, he learns to live with himself.

🚲 DOROTHY LAW NOLTE

Fathers can become frustrated when they play with their child, mostly because they tend to expect too much. They toss the ball, yelling, "Hit it, hit it." But no matter how hard the child tries, he always swings too late. Since we generally spend more time with our child, we are apt to be more realistic about his abilities. Because we watch him and his friends playing side by side, we know that there are certain things that some children do well before their peers, and there are certain things none of them can do simply because they are still too young.

A reminder that every child reaches milestones at his own pace might be necessary to ease Dad's worries that his child is lagging behind (especially when the nextdoor neighbor's child, who is months younger, is hitting home runs).

If I encourage my partner to maintain realistic expectations, he and our child will have more fun together.

. . . love cannot be coerced.

🎋 KATHI MAIO

*W*hen we confuse love with ownership, we're apt to ruin what is most meaningful to us. Instead of allowing the free-flowing spirit of love to take its own course and fill our lives, we demand too much, eventually killing it. This is especially true for young children. They can sense a love that is honest and true; and they can sense when there are stipulations and strings. When we allow them to express their love on their own terms, we are greatly rewarded.

If I love my child freely, my love will be freely returned.

Kind words can be short and easy to speak, but their echoes are truly endless.

𝄞 MOTHER TERESA

Actually, children are wonderfully forgiving. When it starts to seem that every word out of our mouth is harsh, that every answer to his incessant "whys" is an exasperated "I don't know," that all our requests sound like orders and we feel resistance on every front, it's tough to remember all the wisdom, humor, and affection we've dispensed. But our child doesn't forget. He comes to us with another problem to be solved, which we do, and then we tell him, "I love you."

Fortunately, our children remember *everything* we say.

There will be times when I regret the words that come out of my mouth. There will also be times when my words soothe, enlighten, and embrace.

Walking inspires and promotes conversation that is grounded in the body, and so it gives the soul a place where it can thrive.

&🚲 THOMAS MOORE

here are times when we sense our child is troubled. We long to get to the source of his distress, but most likely he doesn't understand his feelings well enough to put them into words. Often a change in surroundings can help. When we venture into nature together, our spirits lift. Attention shifts away from his problems and focuses on the undisturbed beauty around us. Sometimes the words that need to be spoken emerge unprompted and we become privy to important secrets housed within our child's heart.

Whether we talk or remain silent, a walk together helps my child know that I am always ready to listen to what's in his heart.

Do or do not. There is no try.

🐸 YODA

None of us can stand it when our children whine. And for good reason. Not only is it annoying to the ears, but we know that it's often their way of getting us to do things for them. They're afraid to fail or they get frustrated when things don't happen easily enough. Or they may simply need some extra attention.

It is aggravating, but is our behavior much different? If we don't whine, it's because we're better at coming up with excuses. We cover up our fear of failure with logic, while what we should be doing is building our confidence. When our conviction is strong enough, we will take risks that will lead, if not to success, then surely to learning.

When my convictions are strong and I persevere, I can accomplish a great deal.

I wasn't kissing her. I was whispering in her mouth.

🍦 CHICO MARX

Isn't it funny to hear our children talk about sex? With confident authority they talk about "penises" and "baginas," and "vestibules." They make up "facts" about how babies are made and attempt to sound authoritative when describing their own births—they were there, after all! When necessary, we set the record straight. "No, honey, I'm afraid babies do not come out of a mommy's belly button." But, for the most part, we need not correct them. They'll have plenty of time to sort out fact from fancy.

My children are making up their own version of the facts of life. I will enjoy their innocence while it lasts.

Love is blind; friendship closes its eyes.

ANONYMOUS

What do we do when our child becomes friends with someone we don't especially like? As mothers of young children we need to realize that we can't choose all of our children's friends. If our child likes someone, that friend must have some positive traits. Maybe he plays rough, but he's a good listener; the smart aleck might be good at sharing his books and toys.

So we can steer our child and his friend in ways that bring out the best in their friendship. And we can limit negative behaviors by making our house rules clear. For example, "we don't call each other names at our house," or "wrestling is fun as long as no one gets hurt."

I may not be able to change my child's friends, but I can change the way they act in my house.

I like terra firma—the more firma, the less terra.

🐾 GEORGE S. KAUFMAN

A run of dreadful events is always over-whelming. Our husband gets laid off from work; we file for divorce; a friend or relative suddenly passes away. One minute we're sinking in quicksand, the next we're at the top of a roller coaster steeling ourselves for the plunge. Dull is looking good. In fact, dull is looking great. Perhaps we should try lying in a hammock, sipping iced tea, and letting the catastrophies swirl right past us.

After a few "earth-shattering" events, a little rocking and swaying helps me regain my balance.

*I don't think of myself as single. I'm romantically
challenged.*

           STEPHANIE H. PIRO

S
ome of us divorced mothers find ourselves
back in the dating game with several strikes
against us. Our hearts have been wounded—
whether we left the marriage or it left us. Feeling
insecure and unloved, we may be wary of men's
advances, or we may find ourselves responding too
quickly to a bouquet of flowers and a little attention. "Am I ready?" we ask ourselves, wondering if
he might turn out to be a wolf in sheep's clothing.
The first time around we had only ourselves to
think about. Now we have a child or two or three.
That narrows the field significantly. Any new man in
our life is going to have to accept a "package
deal"—the woman he loves *and* her children, who,
at the first opportunity, will remind this newcomer
that he is not their father!

**I may be romantically challenged, but I will meet
the challenge!**

The baby boom generation grew up believing that if boys and girls were raised without gender bias, they would turn out to be wonderfully open-minded adults, combining the best characteristics of both sexes . . . That's often the case, but the path to such enlightened adulthood may be rocky. Even the ardent feminists find their daughters coo over frilly dresses and love their Barbies, while their sons adore fighter jets and turn every stick into a gun.

🚲 MICHAEL CASTLEMAN

Though our generation has been carefully schooled in raising children without gender bias, we are often surprised to discover that biology plays a larger role than we expected. From the onset it's evident that boys and girls *are* different. Without ever having to be taught, our son will pick up a toothbrush, aim, and pull an imaginary trigger, our daughter will turn a dish towel into a tutu and twirl like a prima ballerina.

This makes it all the more important to hug our sons, too, encouraging their warm displays of affection, and climb trees with our daughters, spurring on their sense of freedom and exuberance.

I will enjoy the differences I see in boys and girls, *and* I will challenge them.

Roles

Men are from Mars, women are from Venus.

JOHN GRAY

Not only do we come from different worlds, but we both return to different worlds once we have a child. Our husband goes off to the office while we stay at home, and it becomes harder and harder to relate to each other.

Then, it happens. We are offered a job, our husband decides to return to school, and our roles reverse. Now when we return home at the end of the day, Dad has the same worn expression we used to have when a child's incessant questioning was driving us batty. He clears his throat when we step over dirty laundry en route to the bedroom to change clothes. If we know what's good for us as a couple, we'll use this opportunity to have more empathy for each other, no matter what our contributions.

My partner and I may not always understand each other, but changing roles for a while sure helps bridge the "gender gap."

Temptation

I can resist everything except temptation.

OSCAR WILDE

Children and temptation have a special affinity for each other. They're "partners in crime." A box of cookies left on the counter can't be resisted. A dense thicket that leads to who-knows-where has to be checked out. A piece of gum stuck under a tabletop simply must be examined. It doesn't matter whether we approve or not. It doesn't even matter if there's danger involved. Young children have to explore. As one mother said with a slightly pained expression on her face, "I'd hate to thwart their budding curiosity!"

Yes, young children are innately curious. And it's a good thing, too. How else would they learn about the world firsthand?

My child's curiosity is bound to lead her to temptation. I will learn to regard it as part of the educational process.

Another belief of mine: that everyone else my age is an adult, whereas I am merely in disguise.

MARGARET ATWOOD

Growing up, we imagined that adults knew everything. Now that we're the adults, we can't believe that life is as mysterious as ever. Questions we ask have no single answer; there's no one but us to weigh the merits of each; and we fret over not being up to the task. How did our parents do it? *Did* our parents do it, or was it all a great show?

While it's easy to assume that everybody else knows what they're doing, that everybody else is a real adult, the truth is that there is no magical line to be crossed into adulthood. We may never shed our youthful confusion, and because of that we keep on learning.

Adulthood doesn't necessarily come with age. It can be a stance I cultivate, or a frame of mind.

Boundaries

Let there be spaces in your togetherness.

🌿 KAHLIL GIBRAN

Our young ones, especially if they have siblings, are learning ways to "claim their own space," creating the room they need to express their individuality.

We watch our child's body language change as he establishes himself in each new situation. He tests the parameters of personal space, sometimes defining its boundaries by hitting a friend or stranger who approaches too suddenly. (Clearly, he felt invaded.) Not all children need defined boundaries; some feel comfortable about hugging everybody and inviting people into their personal space.

Whatever our child's preference, we must respect it and allow him the room and boundaries that make him feel secure.

To clearly define my own personal space will help to make my children aware of theirs.

When I stopped seeing my mother with the eyes of a child, I saw the woman who helped me give birth to myself.

🍦 NANCY FRIDAY

*M*ost of us have images of our mother that are larger than life. Through our young eyes, she seemed to be able to do everything at once; she was invincible. Now that we have joined her ranks, we begin to understand how invincible feels from the inside.

For our mothers also, there were tears and anger as well as laughter and joy, even though we may not have witnessed it all. Now knowing what it took for her to perform her great feats, we marvel at what she was able to accomplish.

Knowing that my mother, too, was fallible makes it easier for me to cut myself some slack.

Of course I don't always enjoy being a mother. At those times my husband and I hole up somewhere in the wine country, eat, drink, make mad love and pretend we were born sterile and raise poodles.

🚲 DOROTHY DeBOLT

t's impossible to enjoy parenthood one hundred percent of the time. Honestly, there are times when we don't like it at all. Rather than pulling out our hair or threatening our children, we might instead get away from our children and think like single people.

The first couple of times out, we may not be very successful. We will be tempted to call home every hour to make sure the sitter isn't tied up and the house isn't burning down. But with a little practice, it will get easier. These moments away will revive our spirits, and we may even find ourselves delighted to be coming home to children, not poodles.

To regain my sense of self, *and* my sense of humor, my partner and I must stop being "parents" from time to time.

Flirting is one of life's forces. I wouldn't feel alive without it.

🕯 DARYN STIER

*A*ll of us have times when we feel as if the sensuality of our youth has become history. We recall the days when we were filled with the fresh and poetic passions of a sixteen-year-old. Then, an old boyfriend appears on the scene unexpectedly, reminding us of an adventuresome past. Or, perhaps, someone else's husband flirts with us at a party, stirring up our inner fire. When we get over our initial shock, we discover that the attention feels good. We remember that we are still sexual beings after all. Maybe we'd better rush home and attack our partner before the aroused passion fades!

Flirtation can spark my passions. It is up to me to choose how to direct them.

Faced by immeasurables, people steer their way by magic.

🍦 DENISE SCOTT BROWN

*R*aising children is not a predictable science. There is no standard formula and each child is unique. Although we devise various methods of child rearing based on different philosophies, much of the time we "steer our way by magic." In fact, as we become better acquainted with our child, we may find that the ideas we formulated about mothering before her birth were way off the mark. Frequently, it may feel as though we're groping in the dark, yet somehow we navigate through the rocks and hard places and find the way.

My mothering is touched by magic. I will learn to believe in it.

I notice the girls from Casey's class, who have high standards, peering into their loot bags. They sigh melodramatically and look at me with a kind of pity for my hopeless sense of loot. "Brenda's mother gave out My Li'l Ponies." . . . Well, I'm not Brenda's mother! *I want to announce.* I didn't major in birthday parties. *Instead I merely reach up into my handy cupboard of junk and pull out a magic-slate tic-tactoe. "Oh, I love these," she says, to my relief.*

🚲 MARNI JACKSON

Turning four is a big deal—for our child and us. For one thing, it's the first time we invite our child's friends, instead of ours, to his birthday party. For months he talks about nothing but the big event. We want it to be special for him. But when the day arrives, our child awakes with a fever; the guests get bored with the craft project; the ice-cream cake is too frozen to slice; and everyone ends up fighting over the presents. "Never again," we vow. But most likely number five will be bigger, messier, and even more memorable.

Throwing a party for my child can feel like a game of Russian roulette. Fortunately, the stakes aren't as high.

Insanity is doing the same thing over and over, each time expecting a different result.

ALCOHOLICS ANONYMOUS

*E*ver find yourself bumping into the same old problem, thinking "if I only give it *one* more try . . ." but you keep ending up with the same results? It's like when our young child tries to dig a hole in the sand as the walls collapse with each scoopful removed. Our dogged repetition in the face of hopeless odds is equally absurd, yet we don't see it. Perhaps we need to try some lateral thinking.

Persistence is an admirable quality. So is knowing when *not* to beat a dead horse.

In a game of chess between a father and his eight-year-old daughter, the little girl moved the pawn in the wrong direction.

"You can't do that, Sarah!" Father corrected, returning the pawn. "You have to move forward.*"*

Sarah thought for a moment, walked to the other side of the table—and moved the pawn forward.

—BEN ALGASE

Having children forces us to examine some of our most basic assumptions. As in the game of chess, our rules are so deeply embedded that we can't see beyond the grid they impose on our life. Mistakenly, we assume that everyone plays by these same rules, leaving no room for questions or interpretation. Then a child's simple logic forces us out of our preconceived notion and into a different perspective. What a revelation!

By "bending the rules" my child helps me to question my assumptions. I will remember not to mistake rules for reality.

In every real man a child is hidden that wants to play.

🚲 FRIEDRICH WILHELM NIETZSCHE

*L*ast spring I got up my nerve and enrolled in an improvisation class offered by Stanford University. "Why not?" I thought. At home I'm pretending I'm a talking hand named Hermie or the voice for a stuffed toy named Wizard. How hard could it be?

During my first class the instructor explained, "Most people think of improvisation as performing. It is not. Don't try to be entertaining. Dare to be dull. The most amazing things come from working with what is before you at the moment. Be spontaneous and see what happens."

When it came time to write my term paper on what I had discovered in this course, I could sum it up in one simple statement: I learned to be a child again. Luckily, this time around, I had a chance to do it with adults.

Ordinary play makes extraordinary magic. I can't wait to see what I'll come up with next.

Jealousy

Though jealousy be produced by love, as ashes are by fire, yet jealousy extinguishes love as ashes smother the flame.

MARGUERITE OF NAVARRE

ealousy is a common sentiment among young children. When a new sibling arrives on the scene, suddenly sharing takes on a whole new meaning. No longer the baby, our toddler often feels as though she has to compete for Mom's precious attention. She may experience sadness and loss, and her jealousy may be expressed through angry words: "You don't love me anymore." "I'm going to put you in jail." "You always hold *her*. You *never* hold *me*." For a time, her jealousy gets in the way of developing a loving bond with the new member of the family.

Until our young child is assured of her importance, assured that she is irreplaceable, it isn't easy for her to share something so important: our undivided attention. We may not love her *best,* but we've certainly loved her the longest.

I will be sensitive to my toddler's feelings as she adjusts to her new sibling. She is still learning that I have enough love to go around.

*Mattie was like a rock in the road. You could stare at
her till the cows came home, but it wouldn't budge
the fact of her one inch.*

🍦 BARBARA KINGSOLVER

Our child is persistent. He refuses to understand the meaning of the word "no" (unless, of course, *he's* using it), and he goes after what he wants with intimidating tenacity. We well know the strength of his will. Thus, every time we see that a limit must be set, we have to factor in the cost of the resistance that will follow, avoiding what power struggles we can and bracing ourselves for those we can't.

But a part of us applauds our little one's strength, wearying as it may be. And because of that, we try to find ways to maintain our authority without trampling his spirit.

**A persistent child is often called stubborn; a
persistent adult is considered strong. I'll bear
with the former to wind up with the latter.**

Calvin Coolidge looks as though he had been weaned on a pickle.

      🚲 ALICE ROOSEVELT LONGWORTH

S ome faces don't lie. Children, especially, seem incapable of hiding their mood or disposition. If they don't like a particular food, they grimace, sticking out their tongue for emphasis. When they are frightened or worried about something, the fear is reflected in their face, even when they try to cover it up with a goofy grin.

Mothers can listen with eyes as well as with ears. To know when we've made the right decision about a new baby-sitter or a new school, all we have to do is look. We depend on our skills of perception to read our child's full response to the new situations we both confront.

My child's face can be an accurate barometer of how she feels. It is important to take her feelings into account as I make choices about her life.

There is nothing as eloquent as a rattlesnake's tail.

🪶 NAVAJO PROVERB

Just as we watch our children for behavior that indicates when their mood is souring, we must also learn to watch ourselves. Perhaps we begin to clench our jaw after being asked the same question ten times in a row. Maybe the tone of our voice changes and the volume increases. Or, we may suddenly feel like we're going to dissolve into tears. Like the rattle on a snake's tail, our body's rumblings are telling us we're being pushed too far. Instead of lashing out at our family, it's better to let everyone know that our limit is near.

I, too, sometimes need "time out." I will take responsibility for my moods so that my children need not fear my anger.

The Challenge of Childhood

Happiness is an imaginary condition, formerly often attributed by the living to the dead, now usually attributed by adults to children, and by children to adults.

☞ THOMAS SZASZ

*W*hen we reminisce about growing up, we tend to gloss over the rough spots. We remember our childhood as trouble-free and full of promise. Yet, as one child angrily remarked when his father told him how lucky he was to be young, "It's not as great as you think!"

It's easy to forget how much work is involved in growing up. Our kids seem to play all day, but when we take a closer look, we see that moving from a trike to a two-wheeler and learning how to pump it up a hill can be as stressful as a day at the office. It takes intense concentration and determination for our child to learn how to tie his shoelaces. And important social skills, such as making friends and sharing, aren't mastered overnight.

Childhood can be a magical time, but let's remember that it's also filled with challenge.

I will remind myself that it takes as much courage to be a child as it does to be a grown-up.

Change

It is never too late—in fiction or in life—to revise.

🚲 NANCY THAYER

Change can be frightening in any circumstance, but when we have children, it becomes doubly so. With their well-being at stake, we often feel compelled to maintain the status quo. And while consistency is good, holding onto outmoded patterns is not.

If we aren't happy with the school our child is attending, we should start looking at other schools. If our marriage has become a destructive force, perhaps it would be better for us and our children to start a new life. If we have reached a dead end in our careers, we could entertain other options. We must remember: "It's never too late to revise." And it's those twists of plot that keep life interesting.

My life is a story, one that warrants much editing and rewriting.

Worry

They will judge you as a person who . . . had a light step, a long look, a comfortable way of laughing, who could hoist one into a tree and lift one down again at the right moment, whose coat's shoulder had a particular smell. That is how. I don't think you need worry yourself over that.

SYLVIA TOWNSEND WARNER

others are notorious for worrying. We worry about our child's diet. We worry about pushing her too hard. We worry about letting her fall behind. We worry about when to, and when not to, consult the pediatrician. And by the time she's three or four, we're worrying about our child's perception of us. What we really should be worrying about is how hard we are on ourselves.

I must determine when worrying serves a purpose and when I'm merely spinning my wheels.

Single Friends

When I get together with my childless friends it's like oil and water: We don't mix until things are shaken up a bit.

🍦 SUSAN BOYD

Some of us have friends who are resolutely childless. The only little feet apt to be pattering around their house belong to the cat. Until we come over, that is.

Visits with such friends can be challenging for everyone. Our child, warned about glass vases and china tea sets, seems on a collision course with anything breakable. We hope for a picnic on the lawn, but when we're led to the dining room, we know we'll spend the meal constantly jumping up to save the tablecloth from juice stains. Our friends—accustomed to finishing their sentences—wish we'd relax and share a conversation with them. And it's not much different when they come to visit us.

Mixing family with friends is like riding a roller coaster. I can scream and close my eyes or enjoy the twists and turns of the ride.

Stages

If one stage is driving you crazy, remember: it will pass. Then they'll go through a new phase with something different to drive you crazy.

🚲 HILARY CLARK

*E*ach time our child enters a particularly difficult phase, we begin to think it will never end, as if for eighteen years we'll have to listen to "shut up" and "I don't care." Or for eighteen years she'll insist on following us everywhere, plaintively clinging to us on the few occasions we go out. We feel like captives of emotional terrorism, and all we want to do is run off to a resort, informing the babysitter that we'll return when our child's in college.

It helps to remember that, with time, the undesirable behavior will pass. Of course, we may not be any happier with the new phase she enters.

Each time my child hits one of those more challenging stages, I will take solace in the fact that it won't last forever.

Much serious thought has been devoted to the subject of chocolate: What does chocolate mean? Is the pursuit of chocolate a right or a privilege? Does the notion of chocolate preclude the concept of free will?

— SANDRA BOYNTON

My sister phoned after the holidays, when things had simmered down a bit, so that we could talk at length. It was one of those two-hour communes that ranged from our children to God to movie stars and on to chocolate. "Did you know that chocolate is a natural antidepressant?" she asked. I replied, "All I know is that nothing else satisfies like sitting up at 3:00 A.M. when the house is totally quiet, and I'm curled up with *People* magazine and a box of chocolates." "Thank God you don't have an addiction!" my sister quipped. We both laughed, knowing that, without a doubt, chocolate "precludes the concept of free will."

If I don't indulge now and then, life isn't as sweet.

Out of Sorts

Make no judgments where you have no compassion.

ANNE McCAFFREY

What do we do when another mother complains about our child's behavior? Perhaps our child wasn't sharing during a play date. Or, maybe he was saying hurtful things and excluding other children from a game at school.

While it's normal to feel embarrassed and defensive, it is also essential to put our child's behavior into perspective. Was he up too late the night before? Is he coming down with something? Was it a case of bad chemistry, or just a bad day? These reasons don't excuse his actions, but if our child is acting out of character, we need to know why. And if a new, undesirable pattern of behavior is emerging, we need to acknowledge it in order to help him change it.

The way my child relates to his friends tells me how he is fitting into his world. I will help him make whatever adjustments he needs to continue to be at ease with both.

Partnership

Constant use had not worn ragged the fabric of their friendship.

🚲 DOROTHY PARKER

It is often said that the basis for a strong marriage is to have a solid friendship as its core. Certainly, when one is married, the fabric of the relationship is pushed and pulled in every direction. Teamwork is essential, and each partner must contribute his or her best. When the fabric begins to show signs of wear, both people must be prepared to be a part of the mending process, remembering that each thread is, in the words of Anne Morrow Lindbergh, "fashioned of love."

Caring for my relationship, acknowledging those times when it needs loving repair, strengthens the fabric and keeps it whole.

. . . children are capable, in the midst of the gentlest banter, of twisting one's finger nearly out of its socket, because they have developed their heedless affections on dolls, which never talk back.

🎗 RAINER MARIA RILKE

Youngsters don't know their own strength. Expecting us to laugh, our child bonks us with a toy, and to his astonishment, we recoil in pain. He grabs hold of our hair and climbs up our back as if we were animated characters in the same cartoon. Sometimes, as we gently restrain him and explain, "that hurts Mommy," he seems to understand. That is, until the next time when his exuberance leads to rough and heedless displays of affection.

Later, he'll start using words with greater force, and we may find ourselves nostalgic for these rough-and-tumble days.

I must be patient and firm if I am to teach my child about the use of strength.

Body Awareness

What a difference there is between wearing even the skimpiest bathing suit and wearing nothing! After a few minutes I seem to live in every inch of my body as fully as I usually do in my head and my hands and my heart. I had the fascinating feeling that I could think as easily with my limbs as with my brain.

🍦 DODIE SMITH

In our dualistic culture we don't see ourselves as "thinking with our bodies." Yet, as pregnancy taught us, the body is a wise and knowing instrument that can send out messages telling us to slow down. It performs miracles—from stretching the skin and ligaments to increasing the volume of blood needed to feed the new life inside us.

Now that we are not pregnant, we still need to remain mindful of our body. We need to incorporate the body's special way of knowing into daily life because our wisdom comes from many sources: mind, heart, *and* body.

When I ignore my body or treat it like a machine, I cut myself off from its visceral wisdom.

Denial

Her self-esteem is so fragile, she can't accommodate the truth.

                  🚲 TODD NELSON

*A*t times, our self-esteem is so fragile that it is difficult for us to face the truth. We may be invested in a particular self-image that we are having trouble living up to, and taking an honest look at ourselves means admitting to our shortcomings. For example, a loved one, seeing us pale with fatigue, tells us we need a break. What do we do? We deny it! We like to think of ourselves as strong and capable, and the mere suggestion that we're not becomes threatening.

If we could only step out of ourselves for a moment, we could see that we're being loved, not challenged. And it might then be easier to say, "You're absolutely right. When can you baby-sit?"

Denial precludes change. If I want to grow, I'd better be willing to be a little more honest about my needs.

My husband and I are either going to buy a dog or have a child. We can't decide whether to ruin our carpet or ruin our lives.

🌸 RITA RUDNER

Those of us who chose to become mothers "later in life" have lived enough to know what we were getting into. We waited and waited, wanting to be sure we were ready to make such a lifelong commitment. After watching our friends and sisters juggling the responsibilities of starting a family (perhaps before they were ready), we wanted to make a conscious decision about motherhood rather than leave it to the whim of fate. Certainly, by the time we hit thirty-nine, we should be ready to leave our oat-sowing years and our naivete behind. No one appreciates the awe and the awful of motherhood, like us late-bloomers.

Becoming a mother in my late thirties has allowed me to have my cake and enjoy it too.

It is not a slight thing when they, who are so fresh from God, love us.

🖑 RALPH WALDO EMERSON

Our toddler is growing into a new sense of self—self-awareness, self-restraint, and self-consciousness—making it all the more wonderful when, for no apparent reason, he jumps all over us, squeezes our neck, and covers our face with big, wet kisses. Instead of our sophisticated, worldly-wise little tyke, we see a being "fresh from God" who is overcome by the strength of his emotions. Feeling the power of love, our child is filled with generosity. He has no reservations about showering us with these good feelings, and there are no strings attached. It's as if he brings us a piece of Heaven.

I feel the presence of God in my child's loving embrace. May I help keep the freshness alive.

*For human beings are not so constituted that they
can live without expansion; and if they do not get it
one way, must another, or perish.*

          🚲 MARGARET FULLER

*T*he natural urge of human beings is to expand. If one doubts it for a second, one
simply needs to be around children for awhile.
Not only do children's bodies grow and change,
but their consciousness expands daily, letting in
new insights, grasping abstract concepts, making
judgments, and forming opinions.

An adult's expansion is not so outwardly dramatic. In fact, if we are not attuned to our need for
growth, we may miss a great many opportunities.
For example, we may have a vague itch to take a
pottery class, and when we act on it, we discover
how vitally important art is to our life. Each time we
pay attention to the messages calling for growth, a
new door opens. Remember: It only takes a little
courage to walk through.

Stagnation is death; expansion, life. I choose life.

It's important to our friends to believe that we are reservedly frank with them, and important to friendship that we are not.

🌺 MIGNON MCLAUGHLIN

*D*ifferences between friends are magnified when our children are involved. We may be more flexible with our child, while our friend may insist on keeping hers to a tight schedule. We sit down to dinner with the whole family, while our friend feeds her child early, choosing to eat later with the adults.

It is important to clarify the needs of each family and negotiate compromises before we spend time together as families. However we shouldn't let these occasions stray into comparisons about parenting styles. Some things are better left unsaid.

My friends and I have different ways of navigating through life; that doesn't mean we can't navigate together.

One learns to keep silent and draw one's own conclusions.

♪ CORNELIA OTIS SKINNER

Some topics are worth debating with friends and relatives. Others are better left untouched, and parenting styles is one of them. As one voice of experience reveals: "There is no categorically 'right' or 'wrong' way to raise children. But, if we truly respect our children and tune in to who they are and what they need as individuals, we will know what is best for them *and* what is best for us mothers.

But while it is sometimes wiser to "keep silent and draw one's own conclusions," there is a great deal to be learned from sharing what has worked for us, asking advice from others, and being open to new suggestions. We can embrace a take-what-we-like-and-leave-the-rest attitude, incorporating into our repertoire those new approaches that feel comfortable and rejecting those that do not fit our style.

My style is unique and finds as much expression in my parenting skills as it does in the clothes I wear and the career I choose.

Real vs. Imaginary

*I stopped believing in Santa Claus when I was six.
Mother took me to see him in a department store, and
he asked for my autograph.*

SHIRLEY TEMPLE BLACK

We need not worry about our children being able to distinguish between what is "real" and what is "imaginary." Reality will set in soon enough. And too much literalism can rob our children of the magic of a rich fantasy life before it has time to take root. For this reason, we encourage the belief in certain myths, like Santa Claus or the tooth fairy. We spin elaborate tales around these myths, and we are rewarded by the vivid imaginations of our children. Sooner or later, they will figure out the truth. Hopefully, even though they do, they will retain a belief in magic and in the power of the imagination.

I will see that my child's imagination has time to flourish before he has to face facts.

Disappointment

If this was adulthood, the only improvement she could detect in her situation was that now she could eat dessert without eating her vegetables.

🎐 LISA ALTHER

Children love to accuse adults of always getting to do what they want. After all, from their perspective, adults decide for themselves how many cookies to eat during the day, what T.V. programs they can watch, and even when to put themselves to bed. Adults can even stay up all night. Children look at us longingly and wish for the day when they will be in control of their own lives. Little do they know what we, as mothers do: freedom only seems free in someone else's hands.

Having the power to make decisions is one of the advantages of adulthood. But wouldn't it be nice if sometimes there were no consequences—especially where dessert is concerned?

Reasoning with a child is fine, if you can reach the child's reason without destroying your own.

JOHN MASON BROWN

Those first years certainly kept us on our toes. All the cries and gestures and grunts were so baffling. But we learned more and more about our infant's basic needs and eventually mastered her nonverbal language. Now that our baby has grown into a toddler, we face a different challenge. She not only needs breakfast, but she wants the cereal with the colorful marshmallows that she spots on the grocery shelf. And to a four-year-old, wants are needs. It's up to us to make the distinction for her. Which doesn't always mean saying no. Perhaps we could buy that sugary cereal under the condition that it be eaten only at snack time. That way, both her sweet tooth wants and her nutritional needs may be served.

I know my choices will not always win me popularity, but it's up to me to distinguish between my child's wants and needs.

Masturbation

Children are the sworn enemies of all conventionality.

         🚲 ANONYMOUS

*C*hildren begin to explore their bodies very early in life. Unaware of social mores, they're apt to fondle themselves whenever they like. Pleasurable sensations reward their pursuit, and we know not to pay it too much attention. But when others are around, we become embarrassed, confused. How do we restrain our child without making him feel ashamed?

First we must be clear about what is appropriate and what is not. Then we talk. Hugging and kissing and arm tickling are all fine things to do in public, we explain. While touching private parts should be done in privacy. This is a time when a toddler's room can become his private domain.

If I do not give my children the impression that masturbation is naughty, they will feel at home in their bodies as they learn appropriate boundaries for sexual expression.

A child is fed with milk and praise.

🌺 MARY LAMB

*E*very child learns at his or her own pace. Yet, what do we do when one of our children excels more rapidly in an area than the other? Of course, we will encourage them not to compare themselves. But, as we all know, some comparison is inevitable—if not at home then at school or with relatives.

Perhaps our daughter is a math whiz, while our son has stronger social skills. Instead of accentuating the differences, we can make each child aware of his or her particular strengths. Our daughter is praised for her ability with numbers, while our son is credited with an outstanding ability to relate to others. And, most importantly, we make sure they understand that we value both of them equally.

My children don't have to be the same for me to love them the same. I will celebrate each of my children's gifts.

Children need love, especially when they do not deserve it.

🖋 HAROLD S. HULBERT

Some of us come from households that were ruled by fear. Whatever Mom or Dad said was law, and we could count on the fact that our defiance would be punished. We know how feelings are disregarded in an authoritarian system, and we shudder at the thought of our children coming to fear us.

Because we value our child's individuality and self-expression, we strive for new, more democratic styles of parenting. Yet sometimes democratic measures alone won't win our child's cooperation. We find ourselves pushed to extremes, barking orders, even swatting a bottom. And almost immediately we regret our actions. We hate being unreasonable. We hate having to embarrass our child in front of his friends. We want him to grow up knowing his opinions count. How fortunate that the commander's role feels so uncomfortable, otherwise we might become really good at it.

Company commanders get results in the army, not in my family.

There are certain individuals who, in the process of resolving their own inner conflicts, become paradigms for broader groups.

🚲 ERIK ERIKSON

*E*ven those of us who didn't see *Lorenzo's Oil* know about the real-life husband and wife who were forced to become heroes when they discovered their son suffered from an incurable illness. Unwilling to accept the prognosis, they challenged the medical profession and tirelessly searched until they found their own answer. Then there's the mother whose child was killed by a drunk driver. Wanting no other mother to have to suffer such unnecessary loss, she fought for legislation and founded Mothers Against Drunk Driving (M.A.D.D.).

Most of us will never be called upon to make scientific discoveries or start national organizations on behalf of our children. But it is comforting to know that, if necessary, we, too, can find the courage we need and pave the way for others.

When my convictions are strong and the need is great, I can move mountains.

Sleep Deprivation

Never forget that sleep deprivation is a popular form of torture throughout the world. Its popularity lies in its ability to effectively dismantle an individual's physical, mental, emotional, psychological, and spiritual well-being.

🐾 ANONYMOUS MOTHER

$\mathcal{G}$iving birth the second or third time around can feel like starting over. Except that now, at the end of a night of two-hour intervals of sleep, we are greeted by children already up and on the alert for breakfast *and* attention. Barely noticed are the bags under our eyes!

Soon we stop counting the number of days since we last had a moment of deep, uninterrupted sleep and begin counting the years. Visions of hibernating bears fill our thoughts. We crave sleep the way a starving person craves food. We *need* sleep.

Sleep is essential to my well-being. If I can't get what I need during the night, I need to schedule time to rest during the day.

I have so much to do that I am going to bed.

🍦 SAVOYARD PROVERB

*W*e all remember when working long and hard earned us the right to a break now and then. That was B.C. (Before Children). Now we think wistfully back to the days when we could call in sick at work or skip a class and pull the covers over our head. But, being mothers, we have no such options.

No matter how much we've accomplished during our day, our child still needs us. Dinner has to be organized, bedtime routines must be followed, and plans for the next day have be made. But if we're smart, we'll understand that no one can do everything. We must take advantage of all available help—husbands, friends, grandparents, and baby-sitters—and delegate!

Sometimes the best thing I can do for myself is to accept the help of others. More will get done, and I can let down.

Reject your sense of injury and the injury itself disappears.

🚲 MARK ANTONY

Just because we are mothers doesn't mean we are immune to hurt feelings. Our child has picked up language from the playground or media and can use these words with stinging effect. "Shut up," "I hate you," "You're mean" may merely be ways of expressing her anger or her resistance to what we say, but being our child's target is at best wearying. At times we cannot help taking her harmful words and rejection personally.

While we may pride ourselves on "letting things roll of our backs," it's okay to share our tears or express hurt feelings. How else will our child understand that her words have consequences?

I will show my child that she has the power to hurt and an obligation not to.

It is lack of love for ourselves that inhibits our compassion toward others. If we make friends with ourselves, then there is no obstacle to opening our hearts and minds to others.

PEMA CHODRON

We all sometimes demand too much of ourselves. The pressure to be perfect builds, and whether it comes from within or from without, we resent it. Our resentment grows, invading our thoughts and cutting us off from our hearts. The next thing we know, we're lashing out at someone close to us. Hurt feelings may be fixed with a quick apology, but each time it happens, a bigger toll is taken. Only when we forgive ourselves will we be able to share the generosity of our heart.

Compassion for my family grows in measure when I have compassion for myself.

There's nothing wrong with teenagers that reasoning with them won't aggravate.

🍦 ANONYMOUS

*T*he toddler years are often compared to the teen years—both evoke the asserting of independence and mastery of individual skills. But why is it that they have to be developed in direct opposition to us? At about age three, a simple "no" to a piece of candy is no longer enough. Our child not only asks, "Why not?" but proceeds to detail all the reasons why she should be allowed to have it. In another instance, she wants to ride *on* the shopping cart instead of inside it. When we try to explain to her that it's not safe, she insists, "I can hold on, Mommy. I won't fall off."

Remember when it was possible to walk through a supermarket without engaging in 100 negotiations? But then, if our child wasn't so smart and perceptive, she wouldn't be able to give us such a hard time!

My child needs to test her blossoming self-confidence on someone. Lucky me!

A friend knows how to allow for mere quantity in your talk, and only replies to the quality.

WILLIAM DEAN HOWELLS

*M*others are good listeners. This doesn't mean we have to listen to everything. Sometimes our child needs to chatter away about nothing in particular, and we let him, offering a nod now and then. But we also know when to read between the lines and be sensitive to issues. At those times we promptly drop whatever we're doing to listen carefully to what our child says. Now that's more than being a good mother, that's being a good friend.

I will not only be a good mother to my child, I will also be a good friend.

It is not enough for parents to understand children. They must accord children the privilege of understanding them.

🐾 MILTON R. SAPIRSTEIN

*T*he role of motherhood can force us into a one-dimensional identity: the nurturer who fulfills others' needs. While our role is essential, even commendable, we must be careful not to allow it to be the only identity we give expression to. Otherwise, we will lose contact with other equally valuable aspects of ourselves.

For instance, does our child know we like to dance and sing? Does our husband remember how we used to gaze at the moon for hours and that we love to swim in the dark? If not, our family is missing out on the many facets of our identity, and so are we.

It is a privilege to know and be known by the people I love.

Alexander, your mother is a verb.

ROSE BENSTOCK

*L*ife doesn't stand still, and neither do we. Movement is a part of our nature. If change isn't happening, we'll create it. We prod ourselves and those close to us into action. Even in repose, our friends remark, "I can feel you thinking." It's as though there is a river flowing inside us, and although we may keep the surface calm, the current never slows.

When we direct our movement toward our children by creating a life full of arts-and-crafts projects, baking, story telling, and make-believe, they also enjoy going with the currents of that eternal, inner river.

As an "action Mom" I move things along, setting the pace for childhood fun.

Imagination

I never know how much of what I say is true.

🏈 BETTE MIDLER

Young children have great imaginations. A day at the beach becomes a treasure hunt with pirates. Jewels are found in the sand, and caves in the cliffs house dragons and trolls. If we ask our child any "sensible" questions about his day, we'll probably never know the nitty-gritty of what he did. But does it matter? We can delight in the trip he takes us on.

For my child, each day is an intermingling of fact and fiction. Through him, I expand my version of reality.

Intimacy is not static. It is always moving to a new level. It is an energy flow with no barriers. Intimacy cannot be controlled. Like a feeling, it cannot be reproduced at will. We notice intimacy. We do not produce it.

🌹 ANNE WILSON SCHAEF

Intimacy is a sacred sharing between two people. Sacred because we allow ourselves to be known without pretense. Whenever our partner opens himself to us, we feel a closeness filled with trust and love. Whenever our child confides in us, we are privy to her innermost thoughts. She wants to be known by us and is inviting us into her inner sanctuary. And, in this knowing there's a joining of hearts.

Intimacy—sharing my private thoughts and feelings —is a gift to those I love.

Never allow your child to call you by your first name.
He hasn't known you long enough.

🍦 FRAN LEBOWITZ

*I*t's been "Me, Mommy; you, child" from the start. But then the day comes when our child wants to try out calling us by our first name. Initially, we're amused, which encourages him to press on. He seems so eager to be grown-up that we don't have the heart to stop him. Maybe we've gone back to work and he's trying to connect with the new woman in his life, or maybe he's as tired as we are of hearing the whine of "Mommy." For many of us, however, the charm will wear thin. By then, he may be happy to hear that we'd like our old name back. And even if he doesn't, the phase will pass. Let's hope that the next one is equally harmless.

My child is learning that I have different identities. Connecting with those identities makes him feel grown-up.

Expectations

It is not a bad thing that children should occasionally, and politely, put their parents in their place,

&% COLETTE

From a very young age, our child knows how he likes to be treated. Like us, he needs respect. When we try to make him show off for our friends and family, he may stubbornly resist. When we feel disappointed that others won't see him as we do, or angry because he's making us look bad, we'd be wise to remember that he's no trained seal.

If we think he's wonderful, he'll think he's wonderful. There's time enough for the rest of the world to find it out.

I show my child respect when I allow him to be who he is and let him know that that's enough for me.

Yes, the essence of every love is a child, and it makes no difference at all whether it has ever actually been conceived or born. In the algebra of love, a child is the symbol of the magical sum of two beings.

🌠 MILAN KUNDERA

*A*ll of us have felt this incredible depth of love, "the magical sum of two beings," that coaxed us into becoming parents. Isn't it ironic, then, how the intensity of our love wanes with the introduction of the child into our union. For a time it seems impossible to come together in any meaningful way. In our new roles of "Mom" and "Dad," we focus on tending to details instead of tending to each other. A gulf develops between us. We see it forming, but we feel pulled by too many other needs to overcome it.

But then our child grows and, amazingly, we find ourselves on our own for hours at a time. We suddenly look across the gulf, see our partner staring back, and decide it's time to find our way back to each other.

Rooted in family, the love my partner and I share can be stronger than ever.

Until one is committed there is hesitancy, the chance to draw back, always ineffectiveness. Concerning all acts of initiative (and creation) is one elemental truth: that the moment one definitely commits oneself, then Providence moves too.

JOHANN WOLFGANG VON GOETHE

*P*erhaps we need to take a vacation, but we vacillate, telling ourselves we can't afford it or don't deserve it. Maybe we procrastinate about a job move because we're afraid of making the "wrong" choice. We forget that sometimes any decision is better than no decision at all.

Whenever we resolve to do something, the commitment itself changes everything. Friends offer concrete help. Finances improve. We consider options that before seemed unfeasible.

I must first act, take the risk, before I can expect Providence to move.

Prayer

The healthy and strong individual is the one who asks for help when he needs it. Whether he's got an abscess on his knee or in his soul.

🚴 RONA BARRETT

A mother's life is filled with "close calls," and often we find ourselves praying for help—sometimes under our breath, sometimes out loud. We even use mantras to stabilize ourselves during the more hair-raising encounters.

Our young child wants to cut his own meat, and he ends up cutting his hand. He finds Daddy's razor and decides to have his first shave. Sharp objects are magnets for curiosity. We hide everything, including butter knives, all the while praying he won't discover them.

As a mother, I am relearning the use of prayer—prayers of thanks and prayers for survival.

You look like you have one foot in the grave and the other on a banana peel.

🎖 ANNE WILSON SCHAEF

*E*ver feel as though your life is straight out of the movies—a slapstick comedy, perhaps?

For nights we're up nursing everyone else in the house—a flat tire on the way to the store for juice and aspirin, is a nice touch—then the virus decides it's our turn. Finally, everyone's back on track, and we think we can catch up on our sleep. But the alarm clock accidentally goes off at 4:00 A.M., waking the baby—and once she's up, she's up for good. When we step back and look at the scene, all we can do is laugh and admit, "This is a comedy of errors, and I'm the star."

When I put things in perspective, I can laugh at the absurdity of my daily dramas.

"Just So"

Life is the first gift, love is the second, and understanding the third.

📍 MARGE PIERCY

*W*hen they were little, our children could have cared less about their appearance. In fact, they resisted having their faces washed or they wept heart-wrenching tears when we removed their favorite dirty shirt. What did it matter to them that they looked messy?

Now, as older toddlers, they want everything to look "just so." When we put our daughter's hair in a braid, she wants her bow to match her dress. Our son's football jersey has to be worn with matching pants. Shoelaces have to be tied in a special way—double-knotted, to be exact. They want to look "cool," as if they had a public image to uphold. But, for the life of us, we can't figure out what it is!

My child's sense of style is sometimes a mystery to me. But, if her own unique "look" enhances her self-image, it's worth the aggravation.

A billion dollars is not what it used to be.

🚲 NELSON BUNKER HUNT

Children are expensive. Even a decent salary pales in the face of their needs and wants. It's as if the world turns into one giant store, and we find ourselves repeating over and over, "That's too expensive," which means little to our toddler and makes us feel bad about ourselves. Maybe it's time to acquaint them with one of our favorite pastimes: window shopping. We set aside a special afternoon and hit the streets with our child. When it comes to looking, the sky's the limit. The only rule is that we look only at what we don't need. Our child will enjoy the time spent with us, and we both may find that looking is half the fun.

Sometimes I wish I could buy my child everything he wants. But then what would he have to look forward to?

When a teacher calls a boy by his entire name, it means trouble.

🐾 MARK TWAIN

*Y*oung children know when they're in real trouble. We can yell and scream all we want, but when pushed to the edge, we give birth to a whole new persona, whose presence is larger, whose voice drops lower. Her calm, as she pronounces her child's *full* name, is nearly regal; and she always gets results. Too bad we can't summon her up more often. Of course, then she wouldn't pack such a wallop.

The full measure of my strength will serve me well if I use it only when all else fails.

Confidence

Little did I know, giving birth to my son, the strength I would need to summon, sometimes daily, on his behalf.

🍦 BETH WILSON SAAVEDRA

Sometimes we come up against individuals who feel justified in imposing their views on our child, even though they barely know him. At those times, we must be assertive. For instance, if we take our child to the emergency room because a fever is causing him to hallucinate, and we end up with a doctor who refuses to listen to our concerns, we do not merely bow to his authority. We gather our courage, stand up to the doctor, and ask one question after another until we feel satisfied with his answers and his actions. We may be surprised that we were up to the task. But there's nothing like a surge of personal strength in the face of difficulty to recharge our self-confidence.

Being my child's advocate can pit me against some formidable individuals. But I will remember that no one knows my child like I do.

Standing Up for Himself

I don't blame the elephant for what he did.

🐌 MARLIN PERKINS

*T*hose of us who grew up with T.V.'s *Wild Kingdom* often marveled at the number of miscalculations and foul-ups. We weren't always sure whether Marlin and his team were trying to *capture* the animal or *torture* it. When an elephant threatened to trample the camera crew, we cheered. The truth is, we all sided with the elephant, not the men yanking on ropes and wielding tranquilizer dart guns.

So, when we see others pestering our child or badgering him with taunting words, we empathize when he strikes back. Yet, as responsible parents, we probably say: "No hitting. Use your words." And we hope his words pack as much punch as his fist!

I want my child to be able to stand up for himself. It is up to me to help him learn the best ways of doing that.

Enemies are so stimulating.

🐾 KATHARINE HEPBURN

Some of the more intriguing battles our child will wage are imaginary. We're astounded by the cast of thousands he assembles and by the prowess he demonstrates. A dragon that needs slaying is easily whacked; a troublesome ghost is banished from the castle; a mettlesome alien is always brought to justice. When defeat seems eminent, our child will consult fairy princesses or magic witches or Mom for help in staving off the advancing enemy. His heroic deeds never end. His bravery is limitless. Ahh, the joy of being invincible!

Knowing that one can take on the world—and win—is a feeling I want my child to keep forever.

It is not detaching from the person whom we care about, but the agony of involvement.

AL-ANON MEMBER

As our child faces the mastery of new skills and situations, she experiences a range of emotions. The initial thrill of the challenge may quickly turn to frustration, followed by an overwhelming feeling of "I can't do this."

At times like this it is tempting to take over and complete the task for her. Yet we know we need to allow her the benefit of the struggle. We may have to think up tricks—sitting on our hands or leaving the room at a crucial moment. Yet if she seeks out our help, we are there with help and congratulations for whatever part of the project she was able to complete. And the next time, most likely, she'll be able to push a little further on her own.

Separating myself from my child's struggles allows me to more fully share in her sense of accomplishment.

Affinity

She felt the natural ties of affinity rather than the conventional blind ties of the blood.

🚲 NADINE GORDIMER

*B*ecause an outing to the zoo can be much more fun for us when one of our good friends is along, we take for granted that our child will be equally happy in the company of our friend's child. Often he is, but more and more we're going to find that our child is ready to stretch the boundaries of his small world. He's outgrowing his ready-made playmates. He's no longer shy with children he meets in the park, and at preschool he's learning about partners and buddy systems.

We may be reluctant at first to open ourselves up to these new relationships. Play dates are frought with unknowns and make us long for the ease of our old friendships. But it is exciting to watch our child's growing independence and self-confidence. And, who knows, maybe a day at the zoo with a new friend's mom is just what we need, too.

My child will develop affinities for friends just as I do. I must respect his choices.

Family life! The United Nations is child's play compared to the tugs and splits and need to understand and forgive in any family.

🌟 MAY SARTON

Standing around in the playground one day, I overheard a group of mothers talking. "Do you know why the current family arrangement is called a 'nuclear family'?" one of them asked. The others waited for her response. "Because, with all those people under one roof, there are bound to be explosions!" I laughed along with them as memories of disastrous Thanksgiving dinners, disappointing anniversary celebrations, and chaotic family picnics ran through my mind.

Being mothers *and* daughters, our seat at the negotiating table is guaranteed. Sometimes our skillful diplomacy is enough to bring peace. Sometimes it's wiser to run for cover.

World leaders experienced at handling global crises could learn a few pointers from me.

Only when one is connected to one's own core is one connected to others. And, for me, the core, the inner spring, can best be refound with solitude.

🍦 ANNE MORROW LINDBERGH

*F*rom time to time, we need solitude, a chance to be alone in a place where nothing is asked of us and where the only voice we hear is our own. We find such sanctuary at a secluded beach, a private table at the library, or at a friend's house. Yet, sometimes we don't want to *go* anywhere but simply to have time with our projects, to putter in the kitchen, to have the luxury of being alone in our own home. In short, we want *everyone else* to leave.

It's time to line up an irresistible activity for Dad and the kids—one that lasts all day, and, if possible, all night. There may be nothing as thrilling as being on our own for a full 24 hours—except, perhaps, seeing our child run through the door to greet us on his return.

Sometimes I need to declare my home off-limits to all—whether it's for a couple of hours or days.

*Extra mothering is just that—extra—and babies are
happy to receive and reciprocate it.*

🚲 PENELOPE LEACH

It is common for those of us who've returned
to work to worry. "What if my child forgets
who I am? What if he stops identifying me as his
mother?" We fear that the bond we developed during the first few months of life will be broken and
our child will attach himself to the new person who
sees him through his day—the baby-sitter.

But blood ties run deep. After all, our child spent
nine months inside of us, learning the unique
rhythm of our heartbeat, the sound of our breath,
the sound of our voice . . . He knows who his
mother is. And no matter how much he comes
to love another person and revel in her care, we
can never be replaced.

**I will nurture the privileged bond that exists
between me and my child and be glad that he
is well cared for by others.**

There's nothing more heart-wrenching than to watch good natured fun quickly degenerate into a heated brawl.

🕮 AMANDA PARKER

We hate to admit it, but some siblings just don't get along. Not only that, they don't even seem to like each other. From day one, jealousy and competition have marred their relationship. Even when they accidentally wind up having fun together, something always reminds them that they are not supposed to like each other. And then their game of hide-and-seek is reduced to a wrestling match.

While we can't force them to be friends, we can teach them about respect. We can insist that they treat each other with kindness and allow each other to peaceably go his own way.

My children may not like each other, but they can learn to respect each other. Some day, that respect may grow into friendship.

What we do to the world's body, we do to our own. We are not masters of this world, we participate in its life.
♀ THOMAS MOORE

When a child is given respect for who she is and what she feels, it is not difficult for her to extend this same respect to others and, eventually, to the world around her.

And once she is capable of making the connection between action and consequence, she is ready to understand that something as insignificant as throwing her gum wrapper on the ground shows disrespect for the neighbors, the earth, and for herself. It may require a great deal of demonstration through early childhood, however; and we may find our philosophies put to the test over and over. So over and over, we hold back our annoyance, ask her to pick up the gum wrapper, and point the way to the nearest trash can.

If my child feels a part of the earth, she will treat the earth in the same way that she would like to be treated: with love and respect.

Steve is hypervigilant about not being made into a father figure. Every so often he calls me on this, on my secretly wishing he could be Sam's surrogate father. I always lie at first and insinuate that this is all in his mind, but then I go into another room and all but snap my fingers, like "Rats! Foiled again."

🚲 ANNE LAMOTT

One of the disadvantages of being a single mother is that we're always on the lookout for positive male role models for our child. As a result, we often try to coax our male friends into being surrogate fathers, because we want our child to be exposed to all those wonderful qualities our male friends possess—warmth, kindness, patience, and humor, a different kind of humor from that of a woman. So we find ourselves including our friend in as many family activities as possible, which adds a whole new dimension to our family unit.

I cannot be both mother and father to my child, but I can provide him with exceptional male role models.

Animals are such agreeable friends—they ask no questions, they pass no criticisms.

GEORGE ELIOT

*A*nimals make such good friends. When our children pester them, do they complain? Of course not. They simply move to another room to stay out of reach. Do they scold or reprimand? Nope. Regardless of whether we stroked them before we left earlier in the day, they always wag their tails or jump up into our arms, happy to have us back when we return home. They rarely withhold their love—even if we forget to feed them on occasion. "They ask no questions, they pass no criticisms." What better friend could we wish for?

Animals are great teachers of unconditional and uncomplicated love.

God is not a cosmic bellboy for whom we can press a button to get things done.

HARRY EMERSON FOSDICK

Young children often think of prayer as a button we can press to contact God. While we may teach them to give thanks and express their love through prayer, it isn't long before their little minds bring God down to their level. "If God creates miracles, then why can't God make a new bicycle appear?" they wonder. "If God made stars and planets, then why can't He fill my room with Power Rangers?" It takes our children a while to figure out that God is not synonymous with Santa Claus!

My child learns about magic much sooner than he learns about reverence. I will guide him as he wrestles with the concept of God.

Shop windows display calacas, *the handmade figurines that show a lively afterlife where skeleton musicians continue to play in jazz bands, writers tap their bony fingers on typewriters, and even brides in dresses as white as their bones march down the aisle with skeleton grooms.*

🚴 KATHRYN LASKY

*E*xposing our child to the ways in which different cultures express their spirituality, celebrate life, and ceremonialize death broadens her perspective immeasurably. It helps us, too. These complex topics, regarded with such reverence in our society, are suddenly laced with humor and enlivened with color. Our own vocabulary is enriched by these foreign stories of the soul, and we may even find new answers to some very old questions.

Exposing my child to different cultures will give her a different perspective on life and on death.

You can observe a lot just by watching.

🦁 YOGI BERRA

*M*y friend, Elizabeth, is the mother of a wonderful boy who is considered, by some, to be "slow" because he relies on gestures and facial expressions more than words. Elizabeth is exasperated by the world's constant emphasis on verbal communication. Certainly, language is important, but as Elizabeth can attest: "If you listen with more than your ears, you will hear so much more about what your child is really communicating."

I must learn my child's nonverbal language, which comes as much from his heart and his soul as it does from his intellect.

I can throw a fit. I'm a master at it.

MADONNA

hildren aren't the only ones who throw fits. They're not the only ones who want what they want when they want it. We, too, can lock in on a whim and become totally irrational (not to mention inflexible). Ever notice how stubborn we can become when we've gone too long without doing anything for ourselves? We've been going along, doing everything for the children, then suddenly, it's as if we'll start World War III if we don't get in our work-out at the gym.

When we don't get the relief we need, everyone is subject to our wrath. We need to find proper release valves, or else we'll find ourselves kicking and screaming in a full-fledged temper tantrum.

If I want to save wear and tear on the carpet, I'd better get as good at anticipating my own needs as I am at anticipating everyone else's.

We always deceive ourselves twice about the people we love—first to their advantage, then to their disadvantage.

🚲 ALBERT CAMUS

How many of us, when we first got married, were filled with romantic ideas about the perfect union? Then our white knight reveals his human side and begins to view us as less than perfect, too. We work hard to reach a point of harmony, incorporating or ignoring all those little things that drive us crazy. And then we add a child to the equation.

How lonely it is during those dark moments when we look at our chosen partner and, instead of love and adoration, are filled with regret. Then there are the good moments. We catch him looking up at the sky, explaining to our toddler what makes an airplane fly and our heart melts. Over time, we recognize in our partner a mixture of positive and negative attributes. Hopefully, he can be as generous with us.

I will see my partner's totality rather than focus on the black-and-white perceptions that cause so much grief.

*I don't stand on protocol. If you will just call me
"excellency" it will be okay.*

🏵 HENRY KISSINGER

*I*sn't it funny when our children suddenly
insist on being addressed by an official title.
"You can call me The Queen," our daughter pro-
claims with royal airs. "I'm Master of the Universe,"
our son announces with the authority of a super
hero. Even if it's just a matter of using their full
name—Jonathan rather than Johnny, Jessica instead
of Jess—they want the dignity and distinction that
accompanies such formality. Their new level of
mastery gives them a lofty feeling of being a "big
kid" and, of course, they expect us to respond
accordingly. They may not have access to thrones,
but they can be ruler of our roost. Especially if
Mommy humors them a bit.

**My child won't always feel like "King of the
Mountain," so I'll indulge his sense of self-
importance once in a while.**

Before the child ever gets to school it will have received crucial, almost irrevocable sex education and this will have been taught by the parents, who are not aware of what they are doing.

🍦 MARY S. CALDERONE

Knowing when to introduce our children to sophisticated concepts is not always easy. For one thing, their ability to ask complex questions can exceed their ability to handle the answers. I'll never forget one of my early queries about sex. I naively asked where babies come from, probably expecting a simple answer, like "from my tummy." Instead, my mother launched into a detailed explanation involving sperm and penises and vaginas and fertilized eggs. I listened, rapt.

However, my mother left out one important detail, how the sperm gets into the vagina. For weeks I worried that men could "shoot me with their sperm" from across the street. Finally, I went back to my mother who tried to allay my fears with a complicated discussion on intercourse.

Telling my toddler about the birds and the bees can be risky business. I'd better prepare myself.

I studied those faces, searching for my own image in each of them, but I saw only the tranquil expression of those who have encountered and answered all questions.

🚲 ISABEL ALLENDE

During times of intense change and upheaval, we can feel as though we're the only ones whose life is in disarray. We search others' faces hoping to detect the turmoil beneath their calm exteriors, and when none is revealed, we feel more alone. It is easy to look on others as "having it all together" while we struggle. It's especially important during these times to remember that most everyone has experienced her share of turmoil. Is there someone we can reach out to? We may be surprised by the empathy and understanding we receive.

When facing pain and confusion, I will take comfort in the support of friends and family.

Reality is something you rise above.

🌟 LIZA MINNELLI

otherhood keeps us so busy that we sometimes find it impossible to recall what took place on any given day as weeks, then months, blur together. Things fall through the cracks, unnoticed. When we happen upon old to-do lists, we can't even remember why we planned such activities in the first place. All clues are erased by the march of time, or maybe it's just a case of Mother's Amnesia. Luckily, it's not a fatal disease!

I must remember that it's okay to discard nonessential details, otherwise my brain would explode from overload!

Food is an important part of a balanced diet.

FRAN LEBOWITZ

How many of us forget to eat? We're in such a rush that even when we prepare a hot meal for our little ones, we sometimes forget to include a serving for ourselves. Or, weary of cooking, we find ourselves standing at the kitchen counter snacking on whatever's at hand. That's not so bad if the pantry is full of healthy snacks, but if our shelves are stocked with only cookies and potato chips, we're heading for trouble, especially if we're trying to lose those "last ten pounds." Instead of dieting sensibly, we make up for our splurges by skipping meals, depriving our bodies of essential proteins, vitamins, and minerals that help us to run after children and to think straight. Maybe we need to ask: If we provide our children with three nourishing meals a day, why do we deny ourselves?

I want my child to eat a balanced diet. Why wouldn't I want the same for myself?

Never wrestle with a pig. You get dirty, and besides, the pig likes it.

🚲 CYRUS CHING

S ome people not only enjoy arguing, they revel in it. Those of us who have a spouse or child who fits this description knows what it feels like "to wrestle with a pig." They are not interested in solving problems. Nor do they want to bring an issue to closure. *Au contraire.* They simply love a good fight.

We can easily get drawn into the battle or find ourselves on the defensive, but it is possible to come up with a more effective strategy. Since they're locked into their position, and nothing we say can move them, we can forget about trying to set them straight. Instead, we try working with their feelings. "You sound very angry," we say. "Want to talk about it?" While there are no guarantees that their walls will come down, it will quickly become clear to them that we are not interested in engaging in battle.

If I do not enjoy the fight, I'd better find ways of disarming the contesters.

Oh yeah, it's the 90's . . . People don't apologize anymore.

🎬 KEVIN KLINE

We live in a time when common courtesy and civility have gone the way of Miss Manners. Righteous anger and caustic expletives are the rule of the day.

If we are to teach our child a respect for others, we need to start early. Otherwise, outer influences and what he hears in the street can infuse him with callousness and the attitudes that accompany it. By teaching him the basics of courtesy and good manners we instill the old values of basic human respect.

I will teach my child the value of common courtesy. It will stand him in good stead.

How come my suitcase is so heavy when I'm traveling so light?

🍦 DIANE FASSEL

Sometimes life becomes so full and the need to simplify becomes so pressing that we begin to think about making sweeping changes: getting a job or quitting one, divorcing or moving to a new town. But for those of us who find starting over too daunting or unrealistic, there are smaller steps to be taken.

Sorting through closets, giving away old clothes, or cleaning out the refrigerator can be quite cathartic. From there, we may find the inspiration to call in a part-time housekeeper, ask our baby-sitter for a few extra hours a month, and even stock the freezer with a few T.V. dinners for those nights we can't face cooking. When our load is lightened, it's easier to see things more clearly. We might be amazed at how simple life can be.

Paring down the little day-to-day tasks can simplify my life in a big way.

If you aren't going all the way, why go at all?

                                   JOE NAMATH

*W*hen we were single, we pursued our own personal goals. Now we're furthering the goals of several. Our baby's and toddlers' needs seem to come first as we help them realize many goals. Our husband also needs care and nurturing. And what about ourselves? Little wonder that we long to be caught up in the kind of sensual pleasures that relieve us from the pressures of striving.

But when we or our partners feel we must "go all the way," sex becomes one more goal to be met, and we set ourselves up for disappointment. Instead, we might try suspending our expectations. Perhaps we ask for a back rub; maybe he suggests we shower together as in the good old days. Who knows? Without the pressure of meeting yet another goal, we may be delighted by the outcome.

When I suspend my goals, I make room for spontaneity.

. . . him that I love, I wish to be free—even from me.
        🌺 ANNE MORROW LINDBERGH

Starting kindergarten can be harder on us than on our child. While we know it is a beginning for him, it is, in part, an ending for us. Our child is entering a new phase. His time will be taken over by school activities and greater involvement with friends. Although we will continue to be central to his life, we will no longer be the center of his life.

Luckily it doesn't happen all at once. We can give ourselves time to shed a private tear or two, and we can try including our child in the process. Setting aside a special moment to look through family albums together, tell baby stories, or introduce him to that memory box we're keeping for him can help ease the pain of letting go for both of us.

Assisting my child through life's passages is bittersweet. But, as I begin to let go, we will come to enjoy the next phase of our life together.

You tell me who has to leave the office when the kid bumps his head or slips on a milk carton.

🍦 WENDY WASSERSTEIN

*M*any of us have forged new ground in this parenting game. We are proud that we can count on our spouse to share the day-to-day responsibilities and aggravations of being a parent. However, when an emergency arises, we are *still* the first to be called.

And even if both of us attend our child during a visit to the doctor, chances are the physician will direct her questions to us. Our spouses are certainly capable of handling such things, but why should they when we are so ready, willing, and able to jump in?

If I give my spouse more opportunities to lead the way, we will find ourselves a force of two.

"You almost died," a nurse told her. But that was nonsense. Of course she wouldn't have died; she had children. When you have children, you're obligated to live.

🚲 ANNE TYLER

he depth of commitment we feel as mothers can be sobering. We realize that even on those days when we feel too exhausted to go on we must somehow manage to make it through the day. Conflicts at work or with relationships may trouble us, but we find our personal concerns take a back seat to the job at hand—being a mother. Even when we're ill, we realize that we *have* to get well. Our children are depending on us.

Having children means that I commit myself to life over and over again.

Play

That thrilling free feeling of feeling freewheeling.

🏇 EVE MERRIAM

Nothing is more fun than to abandon all cares and play on the grassy fields in the park. With our children, we turn cartwheels and jump off mounds of dirt. We roll down hills as blades of brown grass catch in our hair. The air is crisp and we smell the earth on our hands. Our feet are bare, our faces red. When the sun sinks below the horizon, we return home, our bodies spent. We will all sleep well tonight.

A day spent playing outside with my child is a day to remember.

*These are not examples of creativity one can point to,
or brag about, or show friends and relatives. Nor the
kind that results in a finished product one can grade,
or make use of, or money on. Just creativity per se,
the* process *of creativity, creativity for the moment,
in all its splendor.*

🍦 MARION COHEN

Creativity is a highly valued attribute. We all
wish we had it, and oftentimes we project
that desire on our child. She picks up a paintbrush,
and we watch to see if a masterpiece will emerge.
She mashes her Play-doh with her fork, and we
commend her on her inventive use of tools.

It is important to encourage our child in her artis-
tic endeavors, but it is also important for us to
expand our definition of "creative." When our child
takes soap bubbles and puts them on her face in
the shape of a beard, that's creative. When she
arranges our jewelry into pleasing patterns on the
carpet, that's creative. And when she tells us about
her day, with a few inventive "embellishments,"
that's creative.

**Creativity cannot be forced, but it will flourish in
my child if I give it the chance.**

The work, once completed, does not need me. The work I'm working on needs my total concentration. The one that's finished doesn't belong to me anymore. It belongs to itself.

           🚲 MAYA ANGELOU

*A*ny work we take seriously requires our full attention. That does not mean we become obsessed with it, excluding all other aspects of our lives. But, it does mean that we concentrate on it intently. We infuse it with enough energy, direction, and shape to enable it to live on its own. Whether it's a job, a novel, or a child.

I breathe life into my work so that it can have a life of its own.

Comfort

Comforter, where, where is your comforting?
GERARD MANLEY HOPKINS

As babies, our children relied on us for comfort. They looked to us to fulfill their needs: rocking them when they cried, soothing them with a lullaby when they were too restless to sleep. Now that our children are older, they often thwart our attempts to comfort them. Our hugs and kisses are treated as intrusions. They want the freedom and independence of being "big girls" and "big boys," and this means that we have to stop "babying" them. Yet, when they are truly hurting inside, they know who to come to for comfort and support. And they know they will always be welcome.

I will remember that my children will never outgrow the comfort only I can give.

Compromise

No partner in a love relationship . . . should feel that he has to give up an essential part of himself to make it viable.

♀ MAY SARTON

*B*eing a mother and a wife often means making sacrifices. We make choices that place our children and spouse first. However, sometimes our relationships demand—whether explicitly or covertly—that we compromise something vital to our well-being, such as our creative endeavors. Perhaps we submerge our own desires and redirect our energies into our family. For a while, this may work. Yet, eventually we'll realize that the sacrifice is too great. When it becomes impossible to incorporate all our needs into the relationship, it is our relationship that may have to change.

I can make compromises, but I cannot compromise myself.

Trust me, but look to thyself.

🚲 IRISH PROVERB

We look to our friends for guidance and to reflect back to us who we are. We trust them to act in our best interests—and they usually do. But sometimes their sense of what's best for us is skewed by their own experience. While their advice is often helpful, we must trust our own counsel above all others. Only we can determine what is the most appropriate course for our life.

I wouldn't expect my friends to live my life for me; neither can I expect them to make life decisions for me.

We see the same colors; we hear the same sounds, but not in the same way.

🦎 SIMONE WEIL

*F*riends do not experience everything in the same way. We don't necessarily have the same taste in art or ice cream. Our political opinions may vary. We are attracted to completely different types of men. We have different theories of child rearing. However, close friends appreciate the ways in which we apprehend the world. They strive to know the hues of the colors we see, the timbres of the sounds we hear, because they love the unique qualities of who we are. We can agree to disagree because the basic connection and love is so strong.

True friends may not experience everything in the same way. Yet, it is these differences that add color and antiphony to the friendship.

Cheerfulness, it would appear, is a matter which depends fully as much on the state of things within, as on the state of things without and around us.

🖛 CHARLOTTE BRONTE

*O*ur perspective has a lot to do with being able to maintain a cheerful attitude. How do we respond to the problems that arise—regard them as burdens, or simply set about the task of solving them? When we encounter the unexpected, do we let it ruin our day, or do we embrace it with a spirit of adventure?

When we're feeling confident and balanced, it's easy to keep our cheer. Members of the family may be grumpy or surly, but we don't have to take it personally. We can take everything in stride. As one mother remarked, "If it's not a crisis, don't make it one."

If I can maintain a balanced perspective, I can remain cheerful through it all.

Among those whom I like or admire, I can find no common denominator, but among those whom I love, I can: all of them make me laugh.

W. H. AUDEN

When I was growing up, errands were never dull. Wherever we were, my father would improvise, going into strange routines that made it impossible for me to keep a straight face. I'll never forget when my parents took me to buy my first bra. The salesclerk, understanding the potential embarrassment of the situation, remained reserved. But above the aisles we could see the bobbing head of a mannequin approaching. Apparently, instead of picking out a few bras for me to try on, my father had decided to bring the whole display for me to examine. Mom and I were practically on the floor, but our poor salesclerk was totally baffled.

That's when I realized that while humor is universal, not everyone laughs at the same things. Those people with whom we can share laughter have special access to our hearts because the world is as wacky and wonderful for them as it is for us.

Laughter shared is laughter multiplied. I love to laugh, and I love those I can laugh with.

*Like a forgotten fire, a childhood can always flare up
again within us.*

🎋 GASTON BACHELARD

S ome of us will go the "store-bought" route.
Others will labor over hand-sewn originals.
Either way, preparing for Halloween can be an
event in itself. For weeks our child will consider
costume possibilities, swinging irresolutely from
Batman to Stretch Armstrong. And despite our
prompting, they remain firmly noncommittal till
the eleventh hour.

But once the witching hour is upon us, the whole
family becomes magically transformed. Dad dresses
up like Mom; Mom dresses up as an alien; even the
baby sprouts floppy ears and whiskers. We get the
family-size trick-or-treat bags, and just the thought
of all that sugar goes straight to our bloodstream.

**Halloween inspires a sense of drama and allows
me the fun of playing dress-up with my child.**

Perhaps the greatest social service that can be rendered by anybody to the country and to humankind is to bring up a family.

🍦 ANONYMOUS

ontributing to a child's life is like no other social service. It means giving to the community of humankind; it means giving to the future.

Most of us have friends who recognize the value of raising children. While they may not have any children of their own, they take it upon themselves to help us with ours. They're part of the fabric of our children's lives, whisking our kids off to the circus, to the park, or to the movies. Do they offer their time out of obligation to us? Certainly not. They forge their own relationships with our children as "aunties," or as "uncles," and best of all, as friends.

I am fortunate to have friends who are an integral part of my children's lives.

Sex is a sacrament.

🚲 STARHAWK

*W*hen my son recently happened to see the preview of a new R-rated film on T.V., I knew it was time for a talk. Fortunately, the part he caught was romantic and loving. But I might not be so lucky next time. Our children encounter such scenes—once reserved for the bedroom—everywhere. They'll see a sexy ad, giggle with embarrassment or, worse, react with disgust, and we want to hide them away until the coast is clear.

But since we can't do that, we should be ready with explanations. Today, it's not enough to hope that our children will grow up knowing that sex is an expression of love.

I will help my child to understand that the world's view of sex is not always an accurate portrayal of love.

If a child lives with approval, he learns to live with himself.

🌺 DOROTHY LAW NOLTE

udgment can deaden the spirit. If our child feels we do not approve of him, he will feel unloved and unworthy of love. For this reason, it's important to separate our child's actions from who he is. By using "I" statements (*"I* don't like it when you say that. It hurts *my* feelings.") instead of "You" statements (*"You* are a such a difficult child. *You're* driving me crazy."), we speak to our child's behavior rather than his worth. In this way, we hold our child responsible for his actions without wounding his self-esteem.

Not only do I want my child to learn to live with himself, I want him to learn to love himself.

Sparking the Soul

The words that enlighten the soul are more precious than jewels.

> HAZRAT INAYAT KHAN

Isn't it wonderful to watch our child's eyes light up as she grasps a new concept! It makes us realize how much of the day we spend chattering or giving directions. But when we do allow our pedestrian concerns to give way to more meaningful moments, the sparks fly. Our child asks a question and we are moved. We work hard to deliver a meaningful answer, carefully choosing our words. And we connect. She mulls over our response, looks up with the glow of understanding, and we know we've struck a chord deep within her.

I will cherish the times my words connect and enliven my child's soul.

Elisa was four when her mother died. At the time, she was stunned and numb. Like most four-year-olds she had little conception of "forever" and could not understand how unalterable death is. A year later, however, Elisa understood that death is a permanent loss, and was upset that she could not remember what her mother looked like.

           🚲 ROB LOUGHRAN

As our child grows older, so does the world around him. Friends move away, treasured toys are outgrown, a grandparent passes away. Our child is more keenly aware of life's events than ever before, but he is not yet prepared for the very real emotions—pain, loss, grief, and fear—that accompany these events.

Most issues we can handle, but when it comes to death, we're short on answers. We're hurting ourselves, and seeing our child's pain makes us feel helpless. We think we must be strong. But our strength is not all he needs. He needs us to wrap him in our arms, hold him tight, share stories about the loved one we miss, and show him that even grown-ups can cry.

The concept of death may be baffling to my child and me, but sharing our sadness will strengthen us both.

The people who say you are not facing reality actually mean that you are not facing their idea of reality. Reality is, above all else, a variable, and nobody is qualified to say that he or she knows exactly what it is. As a matter of fact, with a firm enough commitment, you can sometimes create a reality which did not exist before.

🖋 MARGARET HALSEY

*I*f there is no *one* objective reality—which, by all indications, there seems not to be—why do we often act as if there is? We become so caught up in living a certain type of life that we forget to trust our own instincts. Forever looking outside ourselves for answers, we forget to look within. As a result, we try to force ourselves to believe that "this is the way things are" instead of imagining other options.

When we gain the confidence to follow our hunches, we soon discover that we "create a reality which did not exist before."

Trusting in my own inner reality will illuminate new paths.

The West Africans recognize that to be harsh with a child is to cause its soul to retreat from its body, sometimes just a few feet away, other times many days' walk away.

🍦 CLARISSA PINKOLA ESTES

Some of us grew up in households where harsh words and actions were commonplace. We know how it feels to be the target of blame and anger. We know how it feels to have to hide our hearts, and we vowed that in our own homes things would be different. Yet, now with our own kids, we realize how difficult it is to break these ingrained patterns of behavior.

Berating ourselves for being like our parents only makes us feel guilty and does not lead to positive change. In fact, if we direct our anger inward, it can cause us to perpetuate the very patterns we are trying to break. But if we take a moment to remember how we felt when our "souls retreated from our bodies," we may find we have more compassion for our children and for ourselves.

When I put myself in my children's shoes, I am more mindful of the pain caused by harsh words.

Growing Pains

. . . the most important event in a woman's life is the birth of a child . . . In this period she learns the discipline of sacrifice: her body, her time, her nutrients, her psyche, her knowledge, her skills, her social life, her economic capabilities, her relationships, and her spiritual knowledge and values are all called into service for her children. This passage, ambivalent at best, pushes her to reach far beyond whatever limits she thought she labored within, making her stronger.

🚲 PAULA GUNN ALLEN

As mothers, we are forced to grow in many directions. This process can be uncomfortable and, occasionally, painful as we try to accommodate the challenges of motherhood. Certainly there are moments when we feel bewildered by the dramatic alteration to our life. While, during other phases, we feel comfortable in this new role, thrilled by our triumphs. Yet, no matter how we respond to the many sacrifices we must make, one fact remains: We are deeply changed.

In motherhood I have exceeded the boundaries of the person I always thought I would be.

As the youngsters grow attached to their teachers and classmates . . . they can finally say goodbye to their mothers without reenacting the death scene from Camille.

🌠 SUE MITTENTHAL

For a young child, strides toward independence can be filled with anxiety and drama. Sometimes our children cry because they are truly apprehensive and fearful; other times they cry simply to tug at our heartstrings or because they're not sure what else to do.

Fortunately, preschool introduces our child to adventurous friends who make us seem dull by comparison. His classmates turn towels into capes and leap off playground equipment. He becomes attached to his teacher and is eager to leave for school in the morning to tell her about a new book or a weekend trip.

As these friendships and interests grow, our children are not only less upset when we leave them, they barely notice we're gone.

True independence is hard won. I will cast myself in a supporting role for my child's play.

Who takes the child by the hand takes the mother by the heart.

🍦 GERMAN PROVERB

Certainly we want our parents to bond with our child, yet we may not always agree with their approach. Though we may cringe whenever our parents dredge up another one of those old bromides to use on their grandchild, we don't interfere. If we allow grandparents the chance to establish their own relationship with our child, all of us benefit.

When I step back and watch, I can more fully enjoy the relationship my child shares with her grandparents.

Let us always be open to the miracle of the second chance.

%% REVEREND DAVID STIER

S ome of us didn't have the opportunity to be
the mothers we wanted to be during our
child's first couple of years. Perhaps we weren't
able to spend much time with our baby because of
the need to work outside the home, or maybe we
were involved in caring for an ill parent or a dis-
abled older child, which drained our emotional
resources.

Fortunately, there are second chances. The best
of motherhood is still ahead. We can start anew
with people who can contribute to our child in
positive ways.

**It's never too late to start being the mother I
always hoped to be.**

*Generally, by the time you are Real, most of your
hair has been loved off, and your eyes drop out,
and you get loose in the joints and very shabby. But
these things don't matter at all, because once you are
Real, you can't be ugly, except to people who don't
understand.*

🐰 THE VELVETEEN RABBIT

We live in a very image-conscious society. Slick is in; Real is out. However, more and more, people are beginning to question the nature of beauty. Beauty is evident in the freshness of youth and becomes enhanced with the dignity of years. When we look in the mirror, we may see only exaggerated features, but the people closest to us see our truer self. Whether it's the charm of a crooked smile, the strength of a prominent profile, or a special way of wearing a hat, our authenticity shines through. And those who don't see the beauty of someone who is Real "just don't understand."

**Those who take the time to understand me and
love me, will see the Real, the beautiful me.**

*I live a really good life. I get to meet amazing people.
I get to hang out with the President of the United
States, Okay? I'm the luckiest bitch on the planet.*

🍦 WHOOPI GOLDBERG

$\mathcal{W}$e all experience days when we feel proud
of our accomplishments, incredibly pleased
with the way our life has turned out. We may even
feel a little cocky as we think about how exciting
work is, how we surpassed our greatest aspirations.
We picture the amazing children and friends we
have and say to ourselves, "All these incredible
people love *me*? Damn, I'm good!"

**Like Whoopi Goldberg, there are times when I
~'t quite believe I've reached the top!**

Do everything right, all the time, and the child will prosper. It's as simple as that, except for fate, luck, heredity, chance, and the astrological sign under which the child was born, his order of birth, his first encounter with evil, the girl who jilts him, the war that is being fought when he is a young man, the drugs he may try once or too many times, the friends he makes, how he scores on tests, how well he endures kidding about his shortcomings, how ambitious he becomes, how far he falls behind, circumstantial evidence, ironic perspective, danger when it's least expected, difficulty triumphing over circumstances, people with hidden agendas, and animals with rabies.

ANN BEATTIE

*A*nn Beattie's words will resonate with every mother. No matter how much we may want to, we cannot protect our child from what life and fate deal him. Quickly, we learn the extent of our reach.

If only a mother's love and care were enough.

Every blade of grass has its Angel that bends over it and whispers, "Grow, grow."

THE TALMUD

Mothers are like guardian angels. It begins in utero when we find ourselves talking to our forming baby, urging him in his development, coaxing his presence into the world. After he's born, we bend over him, gently voicing the words of encouragement we think he needs, continually serving up inspiration, propelling him forward, and lending unquestioning support.

In turn, our child is the Angel in our lives. He brings immeasurable joy, irrepressible laughter, honest tears. He embodies life itself: the miracles and the heartaches. He meets life head-on. Hopefully we can do the same.

I am my child's inspiration, and he is mine. We are both blessed.

Index

Acceptance 101
Accomplishments 296
Adulthood, Easing into 189
Affinity 249
Amnesia 265
Anger 128
Anger and Forgiveness 229
Animals 256
Answers 56, 151
Anxiety, Shared 39
Apples and Oranges 35
Arguing 71
Arguments 267
Assumptions 57
Attention 40
Authority 22
Baby-Sitters 252
Balancing Act 4
Beauty 295
Bedtime Battles 111
Being Available 166
Birth 78
Birthdays 195
Bodies 102
Body Awareness 212
    image 59
    wisdom 126
Boundaries 24, 86, 190
Bravery 247
Camping, Then and Now 84
Candor 134

Challenges 230
Change 204
Change and Upheaval. 264
Changing Personalities 7
Childhood, The Challenge of. 203
Child's Dignity 48
        logic 119, 150
        world 30
Choices. 2, 107
Choosing Battles 23
Comfort 72, 277
Commitment. 273
Common Courtesy 268
Communication. 201
Community 165
Community/Friends. 284
Compassion 20, 145, 290
Compromise 278
Confidence 245
Consistency. 174
Contradictions. 57
Conversation 87
Conviction 181
Cooperation. 16, 136
Creating Reality 289
Creativity. 60, 275
Decisions, Decisions 221
Delegating 227
Demands, Multiple 45
Denial 213
Depression. 141
Detachment. 248
Differences. 69
Different Rules 12

Diplomacy 250
Disappointment 220
Discretion 54
Disruption 109
Doldrums, The 43
Double Messages 139
Dreams 76, 176
Earth-Friendly 254
Efficiency 28
Embarrassing Questions 130
Excessive Pragmatism 95
Excursions 51
Expansion 216
Expectations 237
Facts of Life 182
Fairy Tales 103
Family 68
        loyalty 129
        plan 173
        reunions 170
Father Figures 255
Fathers 13
Fathers and Mothers 37
Feeling Fragile 82
Finances 243
First Child, The 31
Five-Year-Olds 117
Flirting 193
Friends 10, 116, 142, 280
Friendship 98, 137
Gender 186
Gentleness 135
Getting Physical 65
Give and Take 160

Goals 270
God. 100
Good Behavior 172
Good Days, Bad Days. 70
Grandparents 293
Greener Grass 164
Growing Up 175
Halloween 283
Healing 47
Heaven and the Heart. 106
Heroes, Everyday 225
Home 61
Housework 44
Humor. 146
Hurt Feelings 228
Illness. 97
Illusions. 162
Illusions of Motherhood 5
Imagination 234
Imitation 53
Independence 292
Influences. 183
Insight 96
Inspiration 298
Interaction 233
Intimacy 235
Jealousy. 199
Joy of Reading 115
"Just So" 242
"Just Watching" 259
Late Motherhood. 214
Lateral Thinking. 196
Laughter, Shared. 19, 282
Learning. 21, 105

Letting Go 271
Life
        choices 34
        purpose 63
Listening 231
Loss 288
Love 77, 94, 133, 178, 215
        marriage, and 238
        respect, and 89
        twenty-four-hour 6
Love's Cycles 261
Magic 194
Magic Words 148
Making Friends 80
Marriage 99
Masturbation 222
"Me First" 157
Mealtime 118
Modesty 66
Motherhood 154, 297
Mothering Styles 67
Mystery 171
Nesting 112
"No" 17
Noise 155
Nourishment 266
Nursing, Extended 108
Out of Sorts 209
Outnumbered 121
Overanalyzing 58
        -extending 42
        -load 163
        -managing 132
Parenthood 192

Parenting 120
Parenting Styles 217, 218, 224
Parents. 144
Partnership 64, 83, 210
Passion. 38
Peace 46
Permissiveness. 158
Persistence. 200
Perspective 32, 147, 258, 281
Pets. 122
Phone, The 159
Picky Eaters 79
Play 104, 198, 274
Playful Arrogance 262
Playing Grown-up 236
Prayer. 240, 257
Privacy 3
Psychic Territory 156
Pushing Too Hard. 177
Questions and Answers 113
Real vs. Imaginary. 219
Receiving. 50
Recharging. 27
Regression 8
Resolve 239
Rituals. 11
Robotics. 36
Role Model 191
Roles. 187
Rules. 197
Safety 138
Second Chances 294
Security 184
Selective Hearing. 41

Self

    -esteem 286
    -expression 232
    -image 127
    -love 152
Sensitivity 62
Setting Limits 26, 244
Sex 29, 74
Sex/Bicycle 73
Sexuality 263, 285
Sharing 15
Shelf Life 9
Shopping 90
Shy Children 75
Siblings 253
    competition 223
    older 88
    rivalry 149
Silence 124
Simplifying Life 269
Single Friends 206
Single Mothers 185
Sisters 33
Sit-Coms 241
Sleep Deprivation 226
Sleeping Alone 25
Soothing Rhythms 1
Sparking the Soul 287
Spirited Children 123
Spirituality 143
Stages 14, 207
Standing Up for Himself 246
Stating the Obvious 81
Stepping Back 272

Strength...211
Success 49
Success Story..55
Summertime 125
Sweet Times 208
Taking Chances......................................140
Teamwork 161
Temper Tantrums....................................260
Temptation 188
Terms of Endearment 93
Time for Mom..251
Transformation......................................153
Traveling...169
True to Ourselves...................................110
Trust...279
Trusting Our Instincts 168
"Use Your Words"....................................167
Values...85, 92
Walking in the Woods................................180
Warning Signs.......................................202
Warrior Mom...18
Women's Magic 114
Words, Power of 131, 179
Work..276
Worry...................................52, 91, 205

Sources

Allende, Isabel. *Eva Luna*. New York: Alfred A. Knopf, Inc., 1988.

Agel, Jerome, and Glanze, Walter. *Pearls of Wisdom: A Harvest of Gems from All Ages*. New York: HarperCollins Publishers, Inc. 1987.

Ames, Louise B. *Your Three Year Old: Friend or Enemy*. New York: Delacorte Press, 1976.

Ames, Louise B., and Ilg, Frances L. *Your Four Year Old: Wild and Wonderful*. New York: Delacorte Press, 1976.

———. *Your Five Year Old: Sunny and Serene*. New York, Delacorte Press, 1979.

———. *Your Six Year Old*. New York, Delacorte Press, 1979.

Andrews, Robert, ed. *The Concise Columbia Dictionary of Quotations*. New York: Columbia University Press, 1990.

Auden, W.H., and Kronenberger, Louis. *The Viking Book of Aphorisms: A Personal Selection* Viking, 1966.

Bepko, Claudia, and Krestan, Jo-Ann. *Singing at the Top of Our Lungs: Women, Love, and Creativity*. New York: HarperCollins Publishers, Inc., 1993.

Berry, Mary Frances. *The Politics of Parenthood: Child Care, Women's Rights, and the Myth of the Good Mother.* New York: Penguin Books, 1993.

Cameron, Julia. *The Artist's Way.* Los Angeles, California: Jeremy P. Tarcher, Inc. (The Putnam Publishing Group), 1992.

Castleman, Michael. "Rambo Boys," *Parenting.* (February 1994).

Donadio, Stephen, et al. *The New York Public Library Book of Twentieth-Century American Quotations.* New York: Warner Books, Inc., 1992.

Elium, Don, and Elium, Jeanne. *Raising a Daughter: Parents and the Awakening of a Healthy Woman.* Berkeley, California: Celestial Arts, 1994.

———. *Raising a Son: Parents and the Making of a Healthy Man.* Hillsboro, Oregon: Beyond Words Publishing, 1992.

Estes, Clarissa Pinkola, Ph.D. *Women Who Run with the Wolves: Myths and Stories of the Wild Woman Archetype.* New York: Ballantine Books, Inc., 1992.

Fitzhenry, Robert I., ed. *Barnes and Noble Book of Quotations.* New York: Barnes and Noble Books (Harper and Row Publishers, Inc.), 1987.

Handley, Helen, and Samelson, Andra, ed. *Child: A Literary Companion*. New York: The Pushcart Press, 1992.

Kingsolver, Barbara. *The Bean Trees*. New York: Harper Perennial, 1989.

———. *Animal Dreams*. New York: Harper Perennial, 1991.

Kurcinka, Mary Sheedy. *Raising Your Spirited Child: A Guide for Parents Whose Child Is More Intense, Sensitive, Perceptive, Persistent, Energetic*. New York: Harper Perennial, 1992.

Leach, Penelope. *Children First: What Our Society Must Do—and Is Doing—for Our Children Today*. New York: Random House, Inc., 1994.

Maggio, Rosalie. *The Beacon Book of Quotations by Women*. Boston: Beacon Press, 1992.

McWilliams, John-Roger, and McWilliams, Peter. *Life 101: Everything We Wish We Had Learned in School but Didn't*. Los Angeles, California: Prelude Press, 1991.

Moore, Thomas. *Care of the Soul: A Guide for Cultivating Depth and Sacredness in Everyday Life*. New York: HarperCollins Publishers, Inc., 1992.

O'Mara, Peggy. *Mothering Magazine*.

Partnow, Elaine, ed. *The New Quotable Woman: From Eve to the Present*. New York: Facts on File, Inc., 1992.

The Quotable Woman. Philadelphia, Pennsylvania: Running Press, 1991.

Paul, Jordan, Ph.D., and Paul, Margaret, Ph.D. *Do I Have To Give Up Me To Be Loved by My Kids?* San Francisco, California: Hazelden (Harper San Francisco), 1993.

Stephens, Autumn. *Untamed Tongues: Wild Words from Wild Women*. Emeryville, California. 1993.